My Browning Family Album

VIVIENNE BROWNING

My Browning Family Album

WITH A FOREWORD BY BEN TRAVERS
AND A POEM BY JACK LINDSAY

Editor: Betty Coley
Librarian, The Armstrong Browning Library

SPRINGWOOD BOOKS

© Vivienne Browning 1979
First published 1979
by Springwood Books Ltd
Bedford Row London
and printed in Great Britain
by Butler & Tanner Ltd
Frome and London
ISBN 0 9059 4722 3

To
DR JOSEPH ARMSTRONG
Founder of the Armstrong Browning Library
Baylor University, Waco, Texas

Contents

All my life I have elected to be poor, and perhaps the reason, or one among other reasons, may be that I have a very particular capacity for being rich.

BROWNING

Foreword

'Browning Societies abound', says Vivienne Browning in her Preface; 'an apparently endless stream of erudite publications on the Brownings currently flows and full-length biographies continue.'

This is no mere additional current to swell that endless stream, with its already boisterous cross-currents of theoretical dogma, argument and (occasionally rather self-assertive) opinion. It is a welcome tributary down which Browning lovers will gratefully turn aside. They will share it with the only survivor of the poet's branch of the family who has bestowed her dedicated and tremendously comprehensive research into his origin, with particular reference to the religious traditions which presented so powerful an influence upon his life and work.

It is helpful and indeed fascinating to be given to realise the perplexities and conflicts which these inherited and complex religious creeds wrought upon the sensitive, searching mind of the great poet, especially since, as we are shown, religion played so great a part in the emotional quandary which for so many years presented its own perplexity and conflict. In the latter part of her Album the author brings her privileged knowledge of Browning's domestic and family relationships to bear upon the dilemma of his frustrated love for Jemima and his sanctifying and perfected love for Elizabeth. Here again this dilemma and its abiding memories are shown to be the inspiration of some of his most beautiful and familiar poems.

To be invited to contribute a foreword to Vivienne Browning's Album is a pleasure I cannot resist, despite the fact that I myself do not possess any qualification or pretension to be regarded as a Browning authority. I am merely a ranker in the army of Browning devotees, enjoying with so many thousands of others, my own personal delectation for this particular poem or that particular excerpt; halted on occasion by the exhilarating duty of searching to appreciate the full interpretation and beauty of some rhapsodical period; and rejoicing with the poet in his prevailing and sometimes underestimated sense of humour, with Fra Lippo Lippi, Dominus Hyacinthus de Archangelis and Pacchiarotto among his foremost attestants.

And it is perhaps appropriate that the writing of this foreword should fall to my lot; because it is not only by the savants but also, and particularly perhaps, by the general run of votaries like myself, that *My Browning Family Album* will, I hope, be welcomed and treasured.

BEN TRAVERS

Preface

Here is my Browning Family Album, comprising a potted Browning saga, family gossip and confidences, personal reminiscences and a collection of photographs of the large Browning family which included the poet Robert Browning as a member of that family.

Not a week passes but Robert and Elizabeth Barrett Browning are written about, talked about, quoted, mentioned and performed on radio and television. Rudolf Besier's play, *The Barretts of Wimpole Street*, is performed by professionals and amateurs. It has been made into a musical, *Robert and Elizabeth*, and films based on the play, made on both sides of the Atlantic, are shown perennially. Duologues based on the Browning love letters and poems are still being written, performed and taken on tour to the remotest of countries. The world, it appears, can never have enough of the romantic love affair of Robert and Elizabeth, culminating as it did in an ideal marriage and the proverbial 'living happily ever after', and giving new life to a bed-ridden spinster who believed herself to be on the brink of death.

As if this were not enough, there is the passionate expression of their love in their own poetry, with heavy drama and conundrums from Robert and love sonnets from Elizabeth, including the incomparable one beginning

How do I love thee? Let me count the ways...

and ending

—and, if God choose,
I shall but love thee better after death.

(No. 43, *Sonnets from the Portuguese*)

For the enlightenment of serious admirers and students of the Browning poetry – and there are thousands spread all over the world – Browning Societies abound, and an apparently endless stream of erudite publications on the Brownings currently flows, and full-length biographies continue.

Two of the largest biographies to have been published in recent years, *The Book, The Ring, and The Poet* by William Irvine and Park Honan (Bodley Head, 1975) and *Browning's Youth* by John Maynard (Harvard University Press, 1975) have been described as definitive. I take this to mean that the literary primary sources and documents available have been exploited, yet reviews of these books state that the real Browning still eludes the biographer. Mystery shrouds the young Browning, his religion, his early love life, the true inspiration for some of his poetry, his dread of being exposed emotionally, the anonymity for his first published poem *Pauline*, his attachment to Hebraism and Hebrew folklore, the lack of reference in later years to the members of the family with whom he grew up, and the insistence on the destruction of his early personal letters and manuscripts. Such mysteries I hope to unveil.

In an appraisal of the recently published *Checklist* (The Browning Institute and Wedgestone Press, 1978, compiled by Philip Kelley and Ronald Hudson) of the total Browning correspondence, William S. Peterson (*Browning Society Notes*, Vol. 8 No. 2, August 1978) points out that in 'what may well prove to be, in the end, the greatest of all collections of Victorian literary correspondence', no fewer than 451 letters to or from Elizabeth Barrett appear before one from Robert, in a chronological sequence of their letters. A few missing letters might be accounted for by her being older than Robert but by far the greatest number of letters missing is due to deliberate destruction by Robert himself and by the recipients of his letters who succumbed to his insistence on covering his tracks. If a reasonable explanation of his behaviour is not made in this Album, I fear that one will never be made.

In his biography John Maynard has referred to the family trees which I have brought up to date over the years, and in appendices has included some family gossip, but being an academic of integrity, he has not accepted anything as fact without documentary evidence to support it. However, in crediting the statements made by my cousin Mrs. Nora Collings and myself, he gives me the necessary cue to make my entrance.

I am not an academic, so don't expect lots of confirmed dates or a work of literary art, but I do have a conscience which urges me to share my knowledge. In this Album I hope to throw light in a few dark corners before it is too late. Destiny, or some Arch-geneth-liac (Browning would call it), placed me in an extraordinary family which produced a famous poet, and selected me to clarify certain complexities arising in the family story. I leave the statistics and verifications to Browning specialists, like Philip Kelley who has already amassed many documents and records of the Browning ancestors, and to Dr. Jack Herring's merry band of students taking 'The Literary Career of Robert Browning' course at the Armstrong Browning Library, which houses a magnificent Browning collection. Dr. Herring confirms he has taught the course about fifty times since coming to Baylor University in 1959, with enrolment of both graduate and undergraduate students averaging thirty. 'All of these students are required to carry out some sort of research project.' These students may be tomorrow's literary critics, and both they and present literary critics can weigh the pros and cons of my story.

As nomadic tribes and ethnic groups have kept alive their history from time immemorial by word of mouth, so by word of mouth our family saga has come down to me through my Dorset ancestors, my grandmother Elizabeth, née Browning, first cousin of the poet, and

ELIZABETH DEACON née BROWNING 1859–1942 and son VYVYAN, born 1895
My grandmother Elizabeth (known as Lizzie to the poet for twenty-nine years) was daughter of Reuben, the poet's favourite uncle.
My father Vyvyan (1895–1942) had a left eye lighter than the right, as can clearly be seen in the photograph. This was a physical trait shared by the poet who had eyes of unequal strength.
This picture shows most directly the author's link with the poet.

my father Vyvyan Deacon. The relationship is virtually only half-relationship, due to the fact that the poet's grandfather married a second time in middle life, and we are descended from the second marriage while the poet is descended from the first marriage, but as I am referring in no way to the genes passed on by these respective wives I drop the 'half' as the Browning genes are undiluted. The poet's grandfather was my great-great-grandfather so that the Browning genes are therefore intact.

The chief testimonial for authenticity lies in the fact my grandmother was thirty when Robert Browning died and she was the daughter of his favourite Uncle Reuben who was only nine years his senior. As I was over twenty-one when my grandmother died, I had a unique opportunity of hearing first-hand stories of the poet as he appeared in small intimate family groups, and of getting to know the family as a whole. After my father died in 1938, my mother married another Browning relative from the 'enemy camp' in a family feud, so that I was able to hear all points of view of Robert in his role as a member of a large family, although my step-grandmother did not know the poet personally.

I repeat the story believing it to be true.

1 · Early Family History

As far back as the parish and county records go, the Brownings of Dorset were inconspicuous God-fearing Christians attending and supporting the local village or parish church, sometimes as churchwardens, but at least one Browning in every generation held a secret – an inherited esoteric knowledge of the early Christian mysteries. This could have been indicated only by scholarship rare in a village community, a gift of healing, possession of strangely-titled books and manuscripts, some in Hebrew, Latin and Greek, in addition to a working knowledge of the Holy Bible.

My father Vyvyan Deacon, a practising medium and lecturer on the Occult and Theosophy, was sole Custodian of the Rosy Cross in Australasia in the 1920s. He gave me religious training from my birth until he died, aged forty-two, in 1938, while I was still at school. He told me he was carrying on the tradition of his grandfather Reuben Browning, the poet's uncle, who was a Rosicrucian, a Christian in the Hermetic tradition, who shared his secret knowledge and training with his nephew Robert.

The secret was well-kept. The only people I have noted who have guessed the secret are Curtis Dahl and Jennifer L. Brewer, who write in their article *Browning's Saul and the Fourfold Vision** (Browning Institute Studies Vol. 3, 1975):

'Though it may not be possible definitely to prove that Browning specifically knew the Hermetic tradition ... it would be highly surprising if he had not been influenced directly or indirectly by it.'

Their definition of Hermetic tradition is so apt for Browning that I quote:

'The phrase "Hermetic tradition" ... refers to a great and partially underground current of Egyptian occult and philosophical wisdom

* Quoted by permission of the Browning Institute, Inc.

taking its name from Thoth, later called Hermes Trismegistus, its supposed author. In its occult elements it flowed down through Neo-platonism, Gnosticism, early Christian heresies, and Cabalism to the Renaissance magic and alchemy of Paracelsus.

Thence it entered the writings of Boehme, Swedenborg, Blake and the English Romantic poets. Elements of it can later be found in Spiritualism and Theosophy. But very early its philosophical ideas became almost inextricably mingled with Platonism.'

After elaborating on the history of Hermetic leterature they write:

'Browning, of course, though he was influenced by Hermetic ideas and used Hermetic imagery, need not have known all this history. However as *Cleon, An Epistle . . . of Karshish*, and *Saul* demonstrate, he would have been particularly interested in the mingling of Greek, Egyptian, and Christian ideas and appearance of "Christian" con-cepts even before the birth of Christ.'

The so-called pre-Christian 'Christian' doctrines were explained by my father as being part of the Divine Paradox which continuously arises in our physical incarnation in the Illusion of Time and Place. They are understood only by those ready to understand them. They include contacting Cosmic Consciousness through Meditation, which induces astral travel and an ability to identify one's self with one's fel-low-men, at which Browning was an adept. By being able to identify with one's fellow-men, one hoped to be able to identify with Christ.

These practices were bequeathed to us by the Egyptians about 1600 BC when life centred around the temples – in barter, social and business transactions, politics, education, healing, and, not least, in communica-tion.

In the place of radio and television, the seers gave news-bulletins telepathically or psychically. If more precise details were required they hypnotised and questioned young boys who then gave accounts of what was happening far away. Similar power was used to heal, in addition to the application of medicinal herbs on which they were experts.

Spiritually developed people of former years were no different from those of today. In discovering the realm of the spirit within, they trans-cended Time and Place. Re-incarnation was generally accepted.

Everything which is experienced is remembered; but recollection is difficult without stimuli or hypnotism. Today hypnotism as therapy is generally accepted. Even the theory that it may be possible to recol-lect previous lives under hypnotism is now being seriously explored on mass media. The idea is new to us. It was not new to the ancient Egyptians, or to the poet Robert Browning.

Re-incarnation could be hereditary memories reawakened, a combination of genes reappearing in the same mixture as before or selection of a particular incarnation by a soul before re-birth. In any case the memory of past experience, whether conscious or unconscious, would provide our conscience or criterion of Morality.

In teaching me such things, and in reading to me aloud from Pythagoras, Blake, Plato, the Bible, and dozens of tomes on comparative religion, from the earliest gods such as Pan – the Egyptian god Min – through every conceivable aspect of philosophy, my father was repeating the sort of thing which went on for centuries in the Browning households between at least one older and one younger member of succeeding generations. It went on specifically between Reuben Browning and his nephew Robert, nine years younger than himself. All the sons who showed interest had esoteric training available. This explains, I hope, the facility the poet had in understanding the people of ancient history as contemporaries and the existence of the extensive Browning library.

In the thirteenth century BC the secrets went with the Israelites in the exodus from Egypt. They descended through the reigns of Saul, David and Solomon; they permeated the rabbinical teachings of Ben Ezra and Hebraic folklore; they enveloped the great Jewish religion extant at the birth of our Lord, Jesus of Nazareth. He entered the Temple at the age of twelve to prepare for his Ministry at the age of thirty. His studies would have included what was later known as the Kabbala, hypnotism, healing, alchemy, astral travel and the Inner Mysteries of the Holy Sacrament.

The Holy Sacrament featured in religions other than Christianity, but during the Last Supper, Jesus made the Holy Communion peculiar to Christianity. It formed an essential ingredient of the Christ living in human form, healing the sick, performing miracles, being despised and rejected of men, withstanding temptation and enduring the tortures of desertion, loneliness and feeling forsaken by God his father, being crucified, dead and buried and rising on the third day from the dead to appear again before man, in his own image or through the guise of another human form. The acceptance of the Holy Communion was an acknowledgment of knowing that one could identify with Christ while confined to the limitations of human flesh.

The Brownings were traditionally the direct heirs of the Christian Mysteries brought over with the chalice containing, legend has it, the

blood of Our Lord and other relics, by Joseph of Arimathea and his
retinue, establishing secret meeting-places in Glastonbury and surrounding villages. They settled down with the descendants of the
builders of Stonehenge and the Druids, who were sympathetic to the
doctrine of Pythagoras, life after death and re-incarnation. Converts
to Christianity were made in a natural takeover from pagan ritual and
temples.

There is no documentary evidence confirming that in the eighth
century Brownings went to the continent of Europe and brought back
first-hand accounts of Charlemagne and his staunch Childe Roland.
Indeed there is no proof that Childe Roland himself ever existed.
Family tradition asserts they were personally involved in the medieval
wars, the adventures giving rise to the Arthurian legends and the quest
for the Holy Grail. Documents I have seen at Winchester showing the
Mediterranean influence on English ecclesiastical art of the time confirms in my own mind the stories my father told me, illustrated by
illuminated manuscripts, of the links between Mediterranean abbeys,
such as at Cefalu, and English abbeys such as Glastonbury, and of
the rites and ceremonies held in the earliest priories of Dorset. I was
told that Brownings, concentrating on the healing of the sick, were
personally linked with the twelfth-century Order of the Knights
Templar, serving abroad, but that they always returned home to Dorset and the surrounding countryside where their name or a corruption
of it can be found in official records throughout the centuries.

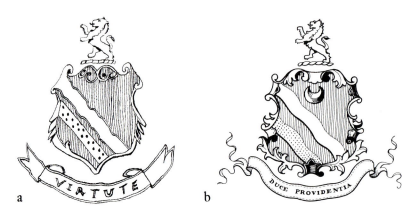

a   b

(a) Rough sketch of Browning crest as used by poet on letters to his first
cousin, Miss Elizabeth Browning, in 1880s.
(b) Reproduction of crest used by William Shergold Browning.

Courtesy of Brian Hulme

They were a motley bunch of ancestors, reputedly including knights rewarded for royal service, and humble tillers of the soil. Armorial bearings in different forms were used by the poet and by William Shergold Browning. Those used by the poet on letters to my grandmother were a lion rampant over a shield and the word VIRTUTE as a motto underneath. Those used by William Shergold bore the words *Duce Providentia* underneath. It was he who, according to Mrs. Sutherland Orr (*Life and Letters of Robert Browning*), passed on 'the now often-repeated stories of their probable ancestors, Micaiah Browning, who distinguished himself at the relief of Derry, and that commander of the ship *Holy Ghost* who conveyed Henry V. to France before the battle of Agincourt, and received the coat-of-arms, with its emblematic waves, in reward for his service.'

There are several possible origins for the bearings, the most likely one linked with the Brownings of Cowley, Gloucestershire.* Royalty could have wished to confer some reward on early Brownings for heroic deeds (as claimed by William Shergold Browning) and the Brownings could have been careless in the use of it, Love and Knowledge being the only wealth they sought, for they were Rosicrucian, meaning 'of the Rosy Cross'.

The rose in ancient Egypt was the symbol of regeneration, or growth of love. To have roses was symbolic of being blessed with love, as in the garden of Midas where grew roses of sixty petals. In Rome a Rosalia Festival was held, and in the Temple of Venus or Aphrodite the rose was symbolic of the stillness of the ecstasy of love.

The cross was the symbol of the descent of spirit through matter, and the Rosy Cross gave it an aura of Divine Love. Some held the rosy cross to be tinged with the blood of Christ. Traditionally Rosicrucians revealed to no man who they were, as from Jesus Himself it was known that he who was ready to receive esoteric knowledge would seek and find and recognise himself in others.

In the seventeenth century the so-called 'Fraternity of the Rosie Cross', rather like the twentieth century Red Cross or Croix Rouge, gave succour to the sick, resulting in miraculous cures. Three of the six rules listed by Francis King (*Ritual Magic in England*, Neville Spearman 1970) are that:

'None of them should profess anything but to cure the sick, and that free of charge.

---

* *Robert Browning's Ancestors* by F. J. Furnivall. A Paper read at the Seventy-second Meeting of the Browning Society, Friday February 28th, 1890.

None of the fraternity should be compelled to wear any particular type of clothing, instead they should adopt the dress of the country in which they were dwelling.

Every Brother of the Order should choose some worthy person to succeed him on his death.'

Secrecy for one hundred years was also advised. From this list one can see that the ceremonial ritual in Roman Catholic services would not be acceptable to Rosicrucians, whereas the simpler services of the Congregational church and Church of England would not be out of place.

Parallel with this fraternity there evolved others linked with Freemasonry both in the scholastic world (in the universities in Germany it involved duelling; see Browning's poems *Before* and *After*), and among the royal heads of Europe. Francis King writes of an independent Rose-Croix which 'was probably under the patronage of Sir Thomas Dunckerly, an illegitimate son of George II, who was also chief of the quasi-masonic Templar encampments.' The reputation of unique powers and knowledge of certain Brownings is supposed to have reached the nobility in these Fraternities in Europe.

Furnivall (*Robert Browning's Ancestors*, the paper already quoted) states that in the early Pentridge (Dorset) registers, 'the earliest entries of the poet's family are the baptisms of four children of a Robert Browning: Elizabeth, Oct. 14, 1719, Thomas and Robert (twins) Oct. 1, 1721, Reuben March 9, 1722.' (Reuben and Christina were regarded as Christian names as Jesus Christ was a Jew, and many Brownings were so christened.) These children were well-educated and traditionally had a library which included a unique collection of medieval medical manuscripts in Latin and illuminated by monks, besides other manuscripts which attracted the interest of visiting notables.

In 1733 a Thomas Browning was granted by the fourth Earl of Shaftesbury a 99-year lease on an old family property, Woodyates Inn. This inn was supposed to be a meeting-place for a Fraternity, sharing their knowledge of religious rites and beliefs involving local significant sites. The hamlet of East Woodyates is near the Dorset–Wiltshire border where Bokerley Ditch and Grim's Ditch, two ancient dikes, are situated; Stonehenge and Glastonbury were easily accessible.*

* The Reverend Anthony J. Lane in his article on 'the brownings at woodyates and pentridge' (*Dorset* (sic); No. 28, Winter 1972) informs us 'that it was at Woodyates Inn, back in 1685, that the luckless Monmouth, fleeing from defeat at Sedgemoor, abandoned his horse, and went on disguised as a shepherd'. He says Woodyates,

THOMAS BROWNING 1721–1794, the poet's great-grandfather. Family heirloom miniature in colour set in old silver brooch.

Thomas Browning, nephew of the above, became in 1760 landlord of the inn, and also keeper of the Poor Box. He was a jovial character given to much philanthropy. He is recorded as having destitute mothers housed at the inn for their confinement and their expenses

'the home of the Browning family for at least three generations has been described in one book on Dorset as being "in the centre of a maze of prehistoric sites" ... Over Woodyates and across the adjoining Oakley Down was fought the battle recorded in 851 in the Anglo-Saxon Chronicle, when Alfred's father, King Aethelwulf, beat the Danes ...' Mr. Lane also writes of an eye-witness account of a visit of George III to the Woodyates Inn which supports the family tradition.

Woodyates Inn

ROBERT BROWNING (1) (1749–1833) was born at Woodyates Inn – of which his father Thomas Browning was granted in 1733 a 99-year lease by the fourth Earl of Shaftesbury (1713–1771). (According to Furnivall this was surrendered in 1760 on the granting of a fresh lease to another member of the family.) Tradition has it that it was patronised by royalty. The inn was situated on the London, Dorchester and Exeter Road, in a desolate place on the Downs.

The photograph is of Woodyates House as it was when it was purchased from the Earl of Shaftesbury in 1947 by the family of R. R. Riddle who writes . . . 'a great deal of the property was built during the nineteenth century, all four sides of the stable yard and the three large central gables were of this period. The further wing facing the main road and the village street may have been earlier but had undergone much alteration.

The oldest part of the main house was a group of four small rooms at the rear of the central gables, these looked out on to the rear garden. The part of the building seen on the top left of the photograph was also very much older, it consisted of the shell of a derelict cottage and included the large chimney stack, the cottage had no room divisions or staircase but had one semi-basement room and an outhouse containing a well.'

My heart breaks when I visualise this old, old room and the history it must have seen, and I wonder was that the room in which the little boy saw George III, on his way to Weymouth, 'aeting 'is paes with 'is fork?

'When Woodyates House was put on the market in 1957, it attracted no purchasers or tenants and when offered for auction in 1964 there were no bids . . . By 1967 we had been advised that parts of the building were a danger to the public, and having spent considerable sums on repairs and upkeep we had no option but to demolish the entire property.'

paid for out of the Poor Box – and this in an inn frequented by Royalty and well before the notorious workhouses depicted by Dickens, which were the usual place for such events. A typically Rosicrucian gesture!

I believe that a kind of Masonic-Rosicrucian nepotism was responsible for the Brownings being educated by the aristocracy and being recommended by them for employment demanding diplomacy, intelligence and a facility for foreign languages. English was their native tongue but in addition to the classical languages for esoteric studies, several members of the family spoke German, French, Spanish or Portuguese or Italian and could read original European literature.

Thomas Browning married Jane Morris (1729–1773) in her home town of Cranborne, Dorset, and brought her home to Woodyates Inn where they produced an eldest son (called Robert of course!) in 1749, and then Elizabeth (1750), Thomas (1753, died young), Reuben (1756) and Christian (1757, who married a William Shergold) and William (1759).

Thomas's son Robert (1749–1833) was recommended by Lord Shaftesbury to a position in the Bank of England, where he remained for over fifty years, becoming Principal of the Bank Stock Office. In the course of duty, as Lieutenant in the Honourable Artillery Company, he helped to defend the Bank in the Gordon Riots of 1780.

In 1778 he married Margaret Tittle, a Creole from the West Indies, whose portrait was painted by Wright of Derby. They lived in London and had three children: Robert (calling the eldest son Robert had become a habit), father of the poet, born July 6, 1782, at Battersea; Margaret Morris (1783) and William (1784 – died in infancy). Their mother died in Camberwell in 1789 and was buried in St. Giles churchyard with her infant son William.

I felt very close to the family who lived in and around Camberwell. My school was the Mary Datchelor School, The Grove, Camberwell, from 1934 until it was evacuated to South Wales when war broke out in 1939. Our school playing fields were at Dulwich, so hundreds of times I walked Lovers Lane and the roads and walks my ancestors and their friends, such as John Ruskin, must have walked. My father died in 1942 in the old St. Giles Hospital, not far from where Margaret Tittle was buried with her baby, making a nostalgic link with the area and the past. I used to look for the graves but I was told that the stones had been removed and the record kept at London's County Hall.

The poet's father was only seven when his mother died. When he was twelve his father married in April 1794 one Jane Smith, in Chelsea. His father was forty-five and his new step-mother a mere twenty-three, so nearer his own age than his father's! They say she was a vixen and had the previous wife's portrait placed out of sight in the attic, but tradition gives the reason for any tension as the jealousy of the father on account of the youth of his new wife. When the step-son was nearing

ROBERT BROWNING 1749–1833 (*left*)

Grandfather of the poet and my great-great-grandfather. He married (1) Margaret Tittle in 1778 (3 children) (2) Jane Smith in 1794 (9 children). He worked in the Bank of England for 40 years having been 'sworn in' August 24 1769.

At the end of his life he said,

'I am a tenant at will, waiting for notice to quit; my lease of life has run out.'

He died at 2 Camden Street, Islington, December 11, 1833.

A memorial brooch containing a lock of his hair entwined with the hair of one William Fleming was left to me by my grandmother as a family heirloom directly form this Robert via Reuben, his son.

Courtesy of Mrs. Nora Collings

MARGARET TITTLE of St. Kitts, 1754–1789 (*right*)

Grandmother of the poet, married to Robert Browning on October 13, 1778. She had three children: Robert, father of poet, born 1782; Margaret Morris, born 1783, who lived in the Browning household until she died, a spinster, in 1858; William, born 1784, who died young.

This portrait was painted by Wright of Derby.

nineteen years of age and the step-mother not yet thirty, it was the old father who wanted the easy-going son far away to manage his dead mother's property in the slave-labouring West Indies. The father could then pre-occupy himself with his new young wife and the family

ROBERT BROWNING 1782–1866

Son of Robert Browning (1749–1833) and Margaret, née Tittle. Married Sarah Anne Wiedemann (died 1849) in Camberwell, February 19, 1811. Two children, Robert, the poet, b. 1812, Sarianna b. 1814.

Worked as reluctant clerk in the Bank of England.

He was primarily bibliophile, cartoonist, caricaturist, versifier.

Joined his wife in worship at the Walworth Chapel where three generations of Brownings were friends of three generations of the Snellgrove family of the Bank of England.

After death of wife was cared for by daughter Sarianna until his death in Paris. Robert, his son, was at his bedside.

of nine children he was going to produce: William Shergold (1797), Christiana (1799), Jane Eliza (1800), Reuben (1803), Mary (1805), Louisa (1807), Thomas (1809), Jemima (1811) and Sarah (1814).

When the charismatic, emotionally bruised young man returned home, after only one year of the nauseating experience in St. Kitts of seeing his swarthy fellow-men, whom he loved to sketch, subjected to the most degrading treatment, his reception was mixed. The young

JANE BROWNING 1800–1880 (*left*)

REUBEN BROWNING 1803–1879 (*right*)
Son of Robert Browning (1749–1833) and his second wife Jane Smith.
Born Kennington, London April 11, 1803. Friend and favourite uncle of the poet who was only nine years his junior.
Reuben took Robert on his first trip abroad, gave him classical books to read, and helped him financially.
Reuben was the centrifugal force of the family at Hatcham – (see Browning Society Notes Volume III, No. 3, December 1973, 'Talking of the Brownings'). In 1846 married Margaret Lewis of Penhelig, Aberdovey, whom he met when she visited London at the age of 20. Visited their beautiful family home in Penhelig, where Reuben painted in water-colours local landscape. Eight children. Worked in the House of Rothschild, St. Swithin's Lane, London.
The family house was called after his wife's home: Penhelig, Morland Road, Croydon, near London.
Humorist, raconteur, artist in oils and water-colours. Mentioned in poet's will. Died September 6, 1879. Obituary in the *Liverpool Journal of Commerce*, Thursday, September 11, 1879.

step-mother had no occasion to dislike the young man whom the two or three toddlers she had at the time would regard as a new uncle rather than a brother, but the insecurity of the father gave vent to a raging hatred of his son, which had the effect of making him meekly submissive.

He accepted philosophically the job his father found for him in the Bank of England, although working as a clerk was a far from natural

MARY BROWNING 1805–1864 (*left*)
Daughter of Robert Browning (1749–1833).
Born March 21, 1805 in Kensington.
Married: (1) Robert Mansir – brother of Louisa Mansir, wife of William Shergold Browning (2) Dr. G. Mason of Lincoln (not known to be related to John Mason, Jane's husband).
Had one son who died young.

LOUISA BROWNING 1807–1887 (*right*)
Louisa, daughter of Robert Browning (1749–1833) and his wife Jane, born April 17, 1807.
Engaged twice but never married.
With younger sister Sarah ran school in Dartmouth Row, Blackheath, financed by father.
Very religious and of great moral strength. With her sister, ethical adviser and matriarchal figure to two younger generations of Brownings.
Lived at the school, then later they shared a home at 32 Maitland Road, Haverstock Hill, near Hampstead Heath, London.
(Mary, widow of Robert Browning of Morley's Hotel is also reported as staying with them.)

JEMIMA BROWNING 1811–1880 (*left*)

Daughter of Robert Browning (1749–1833). Half-aunt to the poet, his closest female relative, being about the same age, and close companion in youth and until her marriage in 1845 to William Hixon.

Had two sons and two daughters.

Eldest son William had a daughter Nora (m. Alfred Collings) who has largest collection of heirlooms from the Hatcham days and earlier, including letter written by Thomas Browning (1721–1794) father of Robert Browning (1749–1833) and grandfather of the poet and my great-great-great-grandfather.

She was beautiful in youth and of pleasing personality, much loved by poet Robert, and by Reuben, whose favourite sister she was.

Born July 7, 1811.

Died November 26, 1880.

SARAH ANN BROWNING 1814–189? (*right*)

Youngest daughter of Robert Browning (1749–1833) born London September 9, 1814. Lived with older sister Louisa with whom she ran a school. She was named after poet's mother, Sarah Ann, and was the same age as Sarianna, the poet's sister.

Was still living in 1890.

occupation for him. He had seen the effect of violence in the West Indies. He found his outlet in sketching and his beloved books. It does credit to the senior staff in the Bank of England that they recognised and encouraged the young man's extraordinary talent at sketching heads of colleagues, hundreds of which survive today.*

When he was twenty-nine in 1811 he married Sarah Ann Wiede-mann who was nearly ten years older than himself and only one year younger than his step-mother. These ages were an important factor in the emotional attitudes developing within this fast-increasing family.

Robert Browning the poet was born on May 7, 1812, and baptised in Walworth Congregational Chapel in a font which I heard recently is still in existence but badly in need of repair as no one appears to claim responsibility for it. A sister Sarianna was born two years later. I vaguely remember my grandmother including a third baby – a girl – in a family tree, but cannot now find any evidence to support this.

The Chapel was the chosen place of worship of the poet's mother. Being older than her placid, indecisive, easy-going husband, it was only natural that she should be the leader of the weekly procession to the Chapel of which she had always been a member and which she per-suaded her husband to join later and indeed to take an active part in its meetings. Colleagues in the Bank of England for more than two generations, the Snellgrove family† regularly attended with them as members, while the rest of the Brownings attended the Church of England.

The regular connection with Walworth Chapel and the sermons of the Rev. Clayton are well-known and recorded, in for instance an article by John Maynard – Robert Browning's Evangelical Heritage (Browning Institute Studies Vol. 3, 1875).

The devout and pious upbringing of the family both at the Chapel and at home by the mother, which was to be remembered and revered by the poet all his life, indicates that there would be little time for the poet to explore deeply another religious practice, but explore it he did, in the family's vast library and in the family tradition with guidance from Uncle William, who later left to work in Paris, and then with his Uncle Reuben.

The Rosicrucian fraternity with its interest in rabbinical folklore was in a position to recommend the Brownings for their employment in the Bank of England; the poet's father, grandfather and his great-uncle Reuben all held positions there. Likewise the linguistically gifted

* For some fine examples see Browning's Old Schoolfellow – the Artistic Relationship of Two Robert Brownings by Jack Herring. Beta Phi Mu, 1972. (Society of Librarians) Pittsburgh, Pennsylvania.

†Descendants of the Snellgroves still retain many Browning letters, autographs, photos, sketches as evidence of their long-standing friendship.

ROBERT BROWNING 1812–1889. Poet. Son of Robert Browning (1782–1866) and Sarah Anna Wiedemann Browning. Born May 7, 1812, at 3 Southampton Street, Peckham.
Moved with family in 1840 to Hatcham, near Uncle Reuben's family.
Married Elizabeth Barret Moulton-Barrett September 12, 1846, at St. Marylebone Church. Lived in Italy until death of Elizabeth in 1861.
Lived with son and sister Sarianna at 19 Warwick Crescent, Paddington. His last home was 29 De Vere Gardens, from which he visited Pen and his wife Fanny in Venice, where he died December 12, 1889.

uncles William Shergold and Reuben (and for a while Uncle Thomas), and Reuben's son Michael, all held positions in the banking empire.

A knowledge of Hebrew was essential for the study of Jewish religious literature. It was also an asset for employment with the leading

SARIANNA BROWNING 1814–1903
Sister of poet. Looked after her father until his death in 1866.
Lived with the poet until his death in 1889.
Lived with her nephew Pen until her death at his home, La Torre All, Antella, near Florence, on April 22, 1903.
Buried in the Protestant cemetery in which her nephew Pen is also buried.

Jewish family in Europe. (The poet's detailed knowledge and use of rabbinical folklore was analysed by Judith Berlin-Lieberman in *Robert Browning and Hebraism*, Jerusalem, 1934.)

Count Corti in *The Rise of the House of Rothschild* (Gollancz, London, 1928) tells of the family's origins in Frankfurt and their rapid rise to fame and fortune in the nineteenth century, negotiating the most important international financial transactions in Europe, and in so doing, mixing socially with the leading families of Europe, many of whom were connected with some branch of Rosicrucianism or Freemasonry. Count Corti records the sending as a representative to England of Nathan 'who did not even know the language of the country to which he was about to travel as a complete stranger'. He says that none of the Rothschilds was a good linguist, yet five Rothschild brothers were established in five different European countries – Amschel Mayer (1773–1855) in Frankfurt, Solomon (1774–1855) Vienna, Nathan (1777–1856) London, Charles (1788–1855) Naples, and James (1792–1868) Paris, and they supported each other in all their undertakings. This seems to echo the several Brownings in their occupations! Count Corti continues, 'Nathan and his brothers made a particular point of letting one another have news as speedily as possible, either directly or through business friends.' One can see how multilingual William Shergold and Reuben Browning were selected for the House of Rothschild Bank in Paris and London respectively. They had heavy demands made on their time for social and diplomatic functions in addition to their routine work, and their many languages were kept in constant use, indeed were a vital part of their work.

The poet's trip to Russia in 1834 was instigated by Reuben, with the assistance of William Shergold, and was a diplomatic mission on behalf of the Rothschilds.

A descendant of Reuben's brother-in-law recalls a large gun which used to hang in their hall. It bore the name 'Baron Rothschild' on a brass nameplate, and was a gift to Reuben. It was given by Reuben to Lewis Lewis before his death.

Reuben's son Michael, born in 1850, was given an elaborate ornamental presentation clock incorporating a bronze figurine. It bore a small silver plaque with the inscription,

Michel Browning
Souvenir de son parrain
1851

and was said to be a gift presented to Reuben for his son by William

Clock presented to Reuben in Paris for his son Michael. The inscription on a silver plaque below the dial reads *Michael Browning, Souvenir de son parrain, 1851.*

Shergold in the presence of members of the Rothschild family and Robert Browning at a social function in Paris during a visit by the poet to Paris in the summer of 1851.

Reuben was the recipient of bequests from Sir Anthony de Rothschild in 1876 and Baron de Rothschild in June 1879. At least two of Reuben's daughters were said to be in receipt of small pensions from the Rothschilds after his death, and Mrs. Nora Collings, granddaughter of Jemina, remembers a descendant of William Shergold Browning, Elizabeth Ann, being a paying guest for a while. 'She was financed by the Rothschilds.'

Reuben's obituary in the *Liverpool Journal of Commerce* (September 11, 1879) included the words, 'He held for sixty years a prominent position in the house of Messrs Rothschild and Sons, who must greatly regret his loss.'

During the 1930s my father used to take me on frequent visits to Tring where he held occult meetings in Champneys, once the property of the Rothschilds, and he spoke of the connections of his grandfather Reuben with the banking family and with politicians of the day, and of the poet's early religious training with Reuben which laid the foundation-stone for all Browning's religious poetry.

This was the background of the poet's life. In his immediate family circle the regular life with simple chapel doctrine, easy-going parents; a lovable eccentric genius for a father, a pious, musical, highly stoic mother, both of them indulgent to their son.

To balance and sometimes in conflict with this he had frequent recourse to a completely different world within the same larger family circle, with the Rosicrucian meetings and in social life with people within the Fraternity.

This gave rise to the religious dilemma expressed in the long poems *Christmas-Eve* and *Easter-Day*.

Secrecy was essential. 'Then charged he his disciples that they should tell no man that he was Jesus the Christ' (Matthew Ch. XVI v. 20) is Our Lord's reminder that the finding of Christ Within, in the Realm of the Spirit, has to be an esoteric subject.

The earliest Christians left fish symbols at the site of their meetings as a sign of their faith. Fifteenth-century German artist Martin Shöndauer, who influenced Dürer, used roses as symbols in his paintings. In similar fashion Robert Browning used the word 'Rose' or 'Roses'. My father said that as a reminder of his faith he used the word 'Rose' more than twice as often as any poet before him. It was 'Roses, roses, all the way,'—not only in love poems as a symbol of love but as in *The Heretic's Tragedy*, where roses in plenty make their appearance; as in stanzas 7 and 8:

7.

Who maketh God's menace an idle word?
  –Saith, it no more means what it proclaims,
Than a damsel's threat to her wanton bird?–
  For she too prattles of ugly names.
  –Saith, he knoweth but one thing,–what he knows?
  That God is good and the rest is breath;

Why else is the same styled, Sharon's rose?
Once a rose, ever a rose, he saith.

Chorus

O, John shall yet find a rose, he saith!

8.

Alack, there be roses and roses, John!
    Some, honeyed of taste like your leman's tongue:
Some, bitter; for why? (roast gayly on!)
    Their tree struck root in devil's dung.
When Paul once reasoned of righteousness
    And of temperance and of judgment to come,
Good Felix trembled, he could no less:
    John, snickering, crook'd his wicked thumb.

Chorus

What cometh to John of the wicked thumb?

This poem was inspired by the burning of Jacques du Bourg-Molay, at Paris in AD 1314; he was the last Grand Master of the Knights Templar.

Many contemporary acquaintances of Robert Browning in his later life lived to span the generation gap to become friends of my father, such as W. B. Yeats and George Russell (A.E.) with whom my father held esoteric meetings at the Abbey Theatre in Dublin and in the New Forest; some of them, like W. B. Yeats and Aleister Crowley, even outlived my father, who died on February 19, 1938. They and other occultists and Theosophists knew that Robert Browning was a Rosicrucian. Those whom I have mentioned were the founder-members of *The Golden Dawn*, an Order founded in Chelsea in the year 1885, a quasi-Rosicrucian order, known to, if not accepted by, Oscar Wilde and Bernard Shaw, with whom my grandmother was acquainted when she lived in Chelsea in 1894-5.

Aleister Crowley – later known as The Beast, or by those who did not know him, a Black Magician – led the opposite faction when the Order of *The Golden Dawn* broke up and Yeats collected his own followers together. Aleister Crowley, knowing Browning's Rosicrucian involvement, quoted him on many occasions in introductions to lectures or small meetings. Using the name H. D. Carr, he published in 1905 *Rosa Inferni* (Neptune Press) with an original composition by Auguste Rodin (with whom the Brownings' son Pen studied sculpture in Paris). It is prefaced with an eight-line quotation from Browning:

ROSA INFERNI

Ha ha! John plucketh now at his rose
To rid himself of a sorrow at heart.
Lo, – petal on petal, fierce rays unclose;
Anther on anther, sharp spikes outstart;
And with blood for dew, the bosom boils;
And a gust of sulphur is all its smell;
And lo, he is horribly in the toils
Of a coal-black giant flower of hell!*

Paracelsus is a poem which is totally in the Hermetic tradition. Berdoe explains at great length and with enthusiastic reverence how this should be regarded the greatest of Browning's poetry. 'It is The Epic of the Healer.' It shows a complete identification of the poet with Paracelsus, the great sixteenth-century healer, mystic, theosophist, student of the Eastern religions, alchemist, who travelled far and wide, acknowledging no social barriers from prince to pauper, almost all-knowing, and yet not knowing enough to avoid coming to grief at the end; in other words, like Browning he poses a philosophical dilemma.

Robert knew that there is a choice of path to follow, just as W. B. Yeats and Crowley later chose different paths, but our poet writes:

Black Arts,
Great Works, the Secret and Sublime, forsooth –
Let others prize: too intimate a tie
Connects me with our God!

Browning was only twenty-two when he started to write this colossus of poems. William Whitla writes, 'Reuben was Robert's favourite uncle. He introduced him to Comte Amédée de Ripert–Montclar, the inspirer of *Paracelsus*, in 1834' (*Browning Society Notes*, Vol. 4 No. 2). Reuben introduced Robert to other members of the fraternity when he took Robert abroad.

* *The Heretic's Tragedy* (verse 9).

Mrs. Sutherland Orr gives Comte Amédée de Ripert–Montclar as the inspiration for the poem, and indeed the poem is dedicated to him. This French Royalist, associated with the Rothschild banking interests and a compatible companion for the poet, would indeed have been interested in and knowledgeable on the lore of Paracelsus, but De Vane points out 'Paracelsus seems to have been already familiar to his father, and several books about him were in the family library'. The fact that the family library contained many ancient tomes on Hermetic lore lends conviction to the idea that Paracelsus is autobiographical in working out religious problems. Robert had been steeped in the Hermetic tradition and knew of the deviation of some of the fraternity, which were reasons enough for him to write the poem, but if one is aware of the affectionate relationship he had with Reuben and Jemima the poem is clear indeed. Reuben, like Festus, was Robert's religious counsellor and friend.

In the poem Paracelsus bids farewell to his dear friends Festus and Michal, and he has a poet friend Aprile. The last is generally supposed to represent Shelley, and the two friends perhaps his father and mother – a view held by biographer Betty Miller, and nearly all agree that Paracelsus is Browning himself. Although there are references which could apply especially to his mother, who used to sing and play the piano to him, I am of the opinion that he made the representation ambiguous in order to deceive, and that many times he is thinking of his uncle and aunt, Reuben and Jemima, when writing of Festus and Michal. For instance Festus says:

> I was born your elder by some years
> Only to watch you fully from the first: ... and
>   ... you left with me
> Our childhood's home *to join the favoured few.*

The italics are mine to indicate reference to joining the Rosicrucian fraternity, and the following could well describe an actual visit to Reuben and Jemima:

> I bear a memory of a pleasant life
> Whose small events I treasure; till one morn
> I ran o'er the *seven little grassy fields,*
> Startling the flocks of nameless birds, to tell
> Poor Festus ...
> I had just determined to become
> The greatest and most glorious man on earth.

Again the italics are mine to indicate the clue that the poet was remembering a visit to Reuben across the fields which he would not have had to cross to visit his father. I will be discussing Jemima in the context of *Paracelsus* later.

The first duty of a Rosicrucian is to administer to the sick and dying. I believe this to be the driving force which urged Robert Browning to love Elizabeth Barrett, who was well-known to be a chronic invalid before he met her, and to pledge his life to her well-being. He did in fact restore her to perfect health in Italy and enabled her to blossom in motherhood, even though she was over forty years of age and addicted to morphine. He weaned her from the drug, and she gave birth to a healthy, bouncing boy, Robert Weidemann Browning, nick-named Pen, who became an artist and died aged sixty-three in 1912.

Robert gave succour to Elizabeth when she was ill, he also tended her when she was dying. As early as 1834 Browning wrote in *Paracelsus*, 'I helped a man to die, some few weeks since,' showing that he knew of the Rosicrucian privilege of being brought to the dying to ease their passing. On June 29, 1861, he was there to help his beloved Elizabeth die, serene and happily cradled in his arms.

In 1866 he recognised the symptoms of his dying father before the doctors did, and his father died lovingly and peacefully with his son tending him.

In 1868 again Robert recognised the gravity of his sister-in-law Arabel Barrett's illness before the doctor did, and again he cradled a dying person in his arms to ease the passing.

> We feel awhile the fluttering pulse, press soft
> The hot brow, look upon the languid eye,
> And thence divine the rest.
>
> (*Paracelsus*)

Reading *Pauline, Sordello, Paracelsus, Saul, A Death in a Desert, Johannes Agricola in Meditation, An Epistle containing the strange medical experience of Karshish the Arab Physician, Cleon* and many other poems of Robert Browning will surely now show that he must have had the deep involvement in a religious order such as I have described.

The Hermetic tradition is understood only by those who recognise it instinctively. I leave exploration of Browning's religious ideals to those readers who are led to discover the truth for themselves, knowing that they will be richer for their quest and will be able to quote from Browning, 'I have lived, seen God's hand throu' a life-time, and *all* was for best.'

2 · *The Rose with a Thorn*

We know the complete love Robert had for Elizabeth from the very first letter he wrote to her in 1845. We do not know from published material of feelings of love experienced by Robert before this time or the dilemma of his emotional experiences from his birth 'with great passion and yellow hair' to the fulfilment of his unique love for Elizabeth.

Robert Browning was born on May 7, 1812. By this time his grandfather's second wife had brought into the world eight of her nine children, the youngest being Jemima, a ten-month-old baby, her eldest sons being fifteen and nine respectively. Mrs. Sutherland Orr writes of the 'friendly terms' between the second mother and the poet's parents and of 'the cordial relations which grew up between themselves and two of her sons', William and Reuben, and later mentions Jemima as being admired by Robert. As happens in large families, these four had an affinity while the rest of the family were taken up with their own problems and interests. Elder sister Jane was perhaps already beginning to store a resentment of the attention given to the baby Jemima and the new young baby Robert, when she herself was approaching puberty, being about twelve years of age at the time of their birth.

William and Reuben were busy with lessons while the two babies were small, but from the moment that Robert could read, he was as much influenced by the books and anecdotes and secrets he shared with the two boys as by his own father in the family library, although the tremendous part his father played in his education is well recorded by biographers as well as by the poet himself (e.g. he records a classics lesson given by his father in his poem *Development* written at the end of his life).

The two families lived just across the river from each other until after the death of the poet's grandfather (1833) when they lived as neighbours in the Camberwell and New Cross area. They shared their weekend and leisure activities – riding, walking, reading aloud, playing music, singing and dancing together – especially as family At-homes were 'de rigueur', and practice makes perfect.

Robert regarded all the children as brothers and sisters but he had a particularly happy brother–sister relationship with Reuben and Jemima which developed after William Shergold married and went to live in Paris, and was well established in the years they were close neighbours, just before Robert began paying his respects at Wimpole Street.

Mrs. Sutherland Orr, who wrote *Life and Letters of Robert Browning* during the poet's lifetime with his knowledge and approval, knew of the closeness of Reuben and Jemima since she heard of it from the lips of Robert himself. Referring to the move of the widow to be nearer the poet's family, she wrote, 'She had then with her only a son and daughter, those known to the poet's friends as Uncle Reuben and Aunt Jemima; respectively nine years and one year older than he.' She then notes that Jemima 'is chiefly remembered as having been very amiable, and in early youth, to use the nephew's words, "as beautiful as the day"'. In contrast with this, W. Hall and H. C. Michin's *Life of Robert Browning* (1910) which relied mainly on memories of the poet's sister Sarianna and son Pen, makes no mention of Jemima at all, which indicates she was someone special and personal to the poet.

My grandmother said that the family grew up bilingual, with French as a second language, because for generations there was a routine whereby only French was spoken in the afternoons and tea-time, at which all the available members of the family would congregate. Because Robert did not go out to work in the day-time, Robert and Jemima would have shared many such afternoons and would have been in the habit of conversing freely with each other in French. This is important to remember when referring later to a French note attached to the first published poem *Pauline*.

Although at times intensely introspective, Robert enjoyed going out with his friends, or with his family to the Dulwich Art Gallery, to the theatre of which his Uncle Reuben was particularly fond, and to the famous Camberwell fairs and gypsy encampments where the young men used to sow their wild oats. He enjoyed his music, dancing and language tutorials and exploring in detail the garden and surrounding fields. He discovered Shelley, who became the major influence on his philosophy until he found that Shelley's doctrine of Free Love with its accompanying irresponsibility was incompatible with his own moral rectitude.

Robert appreciated the nude physical form in painting and

sculpture, as he showed in later life by encouraging his sculptor-painter son to produce such work and then defending his son's work when it was rejected by the London galleries solely for the nudity of the subject. But in private Robert was modest all his life, and held the Victorian preference for a private dressing room in his home. When he was a small child he crawled on a meandering course on all fours to avoid being seen scantily-dressed in the mirror by visitors in the drawing-room. The poet's modesty and rigid self-discipline were in-stilled into me as a child. Although other members of the family were equally self-disciplined it was essential that I should bear this in mind.

When he was sixteen, in 1828, Robert's father entered him at University College, London University (being newly-formed to cater for Dissenters), but it was not long before the poet abandoned that way of life. He was homesick. He loved and adored his mother, as normal boys do, but he must have been homesick for other things as well as for his parents. Any attempt to make out that he had an overwhelming mother-complex which precluded any heterosexual attachment up to an age beyond thirty, falls down when one understands the poet as a human being.

The relationship between his parents and himself could not have been better. After the initial alarm at his Shelleyian rebellion against her church and the Rev. Clayton's sermons, his mother coped philo-sophically and good-humouredly with his atheism, vegetarianism and enthusiastic hero-worship of his idol. Both parents were what today would be called 'regular' and consistently permissive.

As for his understanding the physical expression of love towards the opposite sex, one can see he idealised the experience, vide the open-ing lines of *Pauline*:

> Pauline, mine own, bend o'er me – thy soft breast
> Shall pant to mine – bend o'er me – thy sweet eyes,
> And loosened hair, and breathing lips, and arms
> Drawing me to thee – these build up a screen
> To shut me in with thee, and from all fear, . . .

The incongruity lies in the number of experiences of unrequited love and lack of fulfilment of such relationships which appear in his early poems, when one knows that a young man of his social graces, honesty, charm and vitality should never have experienced such reactions nor have felt obliged to express them constantly.

When at university he must have missed his study-bedroom with its powerful picture of Perseus and Andromeda on the wall – his favourite print of an engraving by Giovanni Volpate, 1772, of the fresco by Polidoro da Caravaggio;* it appears in his first published poem, *Pauline*. He must have missed the wonderful facilities for private study indoors with the family library, and the glorious natural surroundings out-of-doors, with its varied landscape, full of flora and fauna to capture the imagination and heart of a young poet. He must have missed the carefree times he shared with Jemima, the girl he grew up with to know as a dear playmate.

In literature on Browning the Perseus and Andromeda picture has been referred to as representing the rescue of Elizabeth from Wimpole Street, but it represented many phases of emotion in his struggle with religion and love from early years to death.

John Maynard quotes from the ending of *Pauline*:

> As she awaits the snake on the wet beach,
> By the dark rock, and the white wave just breaking
> At her feet; quite naked and alone, – a thing
> You doubt not, nor fear for, secure that God
> Will come in thunder from the stars to save her ...

and continues: 'Changeless in the pose in which the artist has captured her, she is yet within a threatening, emotionally, even sexually charged landscape where movement and contrasts of dark and light wage an endless contest against the larger controlling vision of the artist.'

In such an atmosphere he would have spent time with Jemima of whom he wrote in a letter to Michael Field† that 'the most beautiful woman he ever saw was two years older than himself and for all that his aunt, his grandfather having married a second time in middle life'.

Robert's error in her age by one year is typical of his referring to ages and dates mistakenly. He was aware that time is but an illusion and that character, emotions and passions were of prime importance. The main thing to note is that he seldom referred to his aunt and as far as I know he did not make a similar remark about any other female playmate or friend of his youth; Jemima's granddaughter Mrs. Nora Collings remembers the family story that Robert was in love with his aunt Jemima.

The subject of Browning's poem *Pauline* could not be anyone other than Jemima! The poem was published secretly and anonymously at

* See pp. 160–161 of John Maynard's *Browning's Youth*.
† *Browning Society Notes*, Vol. 3, December 1973.

the poet's own expense* with money given to him by his maternal aunt. The full title was *Pauline; A fragment of a confession*, and to it was pinned a note in French purported to have been signed by Pauline. It was also prefaced by a note in Latin from *H. Cor. Agrippa De Occult. Phil.*

I am no literary critic so I leave the final analysis to the experts, but, given that Jemima *was* Browning's first love and Pauline, to me that fragment of a strange and wonderful poem, with those particular appendages, indicates the most poignant story imaginable of a young man who is suddenly aware that his childhood companion is transformed into a beautiful young woman who stirs in him his first adult passions, alternately pleasurable and agonising, finding that sometimes they are reciprocated in kind, sometimes not at all. Then comes the dreadful realisation that this wonderful new feeling of overwhelming love is unacceptable in a civilised world. The boy who could have everything his heart desired is suddenly smitten with anguish at not only being unable to give vent fully to his passion, but having to keep his feelings secret, yet give the outward appearance that his friendship with this lovely girl has not undergone a crisis! What a weight of guilt, torment and confusion for a handsome youth to have to bear! What a dilemma for a young man who had pledged his life to endeavouring to be a Christian as exemplified in the life of Jesus Christ! How could he fight this problem? Could he sublimate this feeling of love, or should he kill it by suppression in his mind? Never once did he, could he feel that this love was not beautiful, he could only know that it could not find fulfilment in marriage; and yet if she were not his blood relation he could have married her.

I see the young poet sitting in front of his picture of Perseus and Andromeda, she chained helplessly to the rock and Perseus about to slay the threatening monster at his feet, but how ironic that it all has to stay in suspended animation. The picture remains forever in that same state. In real life one has to strive to resolve such a situation. In front of this picture the poet would sit and see a procession of monsters as he worked out his feelings about Shelley, about religion, about the tormenting irreconcilable feelings of passionate love, some to be discussed with Reuben and some with Jemima and all, all worked out compulsively on paper in a torrential outburst of poetry.

His mother and father were proud of his poetical efforts – why did they not have the option of publishing his first poem? Could a young man let his mother see his passionate outpourings when she might

* By Saunders and Otley, Conduit Street, in 1833.

guess who inspired them? Why was it only a fragment? – and why use a subterfuge of an appendage in French and one in Latin? – and after going to all that trouble over camouflage, why resort to absolute secrecy? French was a language he shared with Jemima, and if he had expressed fully his feelings about her there would have had to be drastic cutting – hence the fragment. Yet with so much life-blood poured into the creation, what could be left should remain and Jemima would advise its publication. The Latin refers to the probability that inquisitive readers will cry out that 'we are teaching forbidden things', and announces that 'the gate of Hell is in this book', and ends by asking readers to forgive his youth. Browning was twenty when he completed the poem. The French prose argues whether the poem merits preservation or burning and Pauline decides in favour of preservation as others besides herself see merits in it. I believe that Jemima helped to edit the parts which could be published without suspicion and that Reuben might even have been consulted. If this was the case then there is no mystery. It explains why the personification of Pauline was left so much in doubt as to cause the critics to bicker and argue throughout a long procession of volumes over the past one hundred and fifty years as to who Pauline was, *if* she was!

Mrs. Sutherland Orr in *A Handbook to the Works of Robert Browning* (1885) believed Pauline to be Eliza Flower 'in spite of the poet's denials'. Eliza was nine years older than the poet, the same age as Reuben, and was one of two sisters with whom the young poet as a lad had a sincere and intellectual friendship. The other sister Sarah composed the hymn 'Nearer my God to thee', and both of them afforded the young boy a ready outlet for his earliest verse, which he endeavoured later to destroy completely and for the most part succeeded. He upset the religious sisters when he became a disciple of Shelley. He was genuinely fond of them and was very upset to learn of Eliza's death in 1846, at the age of forty-three. Surely Robert would have no need to deny that this dear friend had inspired him to write purely imaginative romantic poetry? Few people support this claim as being more than a possibility.

Edward Berdoe (1912) in *The Browning Cyclopaedia* is not so rash as to argue with what his poet writes. He states plainly that 'The poem is a fragment of a confession from a young man to a young woman whom he loves ... It is the revelation of a soul ... terrified at its own vast shadow, fearing to face its own spectres, and instinctively "building up a screen" of woman's love to be shut in with from a brood of fancies with which he dare not wrestle. ... He is sure of her love though

ghosts of the past haunt them.' Berdoe does not make so bold as to
suggest someone as Pauline or to attempt to interpret the poet.

De Vane in *A Browning Handbook* (1955) – a book which I admire
and use as constant companion – dismisses Pauline as mere fantasy.
He prosaically gives the true facts, that Browning recorded the evening
of October 22 as being the date of the conception of the idea of Pauline
after seeing Edmund Kean acting in Richmond in *Richard III*. He
also notes that Browning was but twenty years of age and the imaginary
subject of the poem was of that age. Neither of these statements jus-
tifies in my mind Browning's denials and the embarrassment felt by
him for decades to come. De Vane quotes Mrs. Sutherland Orr, 'If,
in spite of his denials ... any woman inspired *Pauline*, it can be none
other than she', i.e. Eliza Flower and states, 'This is probably true,
but that Browning was passionately in love with any woman at the
time can hardly be deduced from the poem.' He goes on to quote John
Stuart Mill, 'If she *existed* and loved him, he treats her most ungener-
ously and unfeelingly.'

De Vane states that 'The real matter of *Pauline* is Browning's
struggle with his religious skepticism between the years of 1826 and
1832.'

He gives a thorough analysis of the poem, and the facts of Browning's fanatical desire for anonymity, and the extent to which he went
to preserve it, but gives no logical explanation as to why he was thus
possessed or why the poem should be but a fragment or deal with a
named woman Pauline at all, whether figuratively or really. No reason
is given for his embarrassment or for not reprinting it until 1868, seven
years after the death of Elizabeth when the subject would no longer
be dynamite.

If Pauline was not Jemima – or any living creature – why did Robert
revive the pseudonym in another poem? In *One Way of Love* he writes:

> All June I bound the rose in sheaves
> Now, rose by rose, I strip the leaves
> And strew them where Pauline may pass.
> She will not turn aside? Alas!
> Let them lie. Suppose they die?
> The chance was they might take her eye.

Isn't this just like a Personal Column entry in the press? – An explanation that he has bound up his loving thoughts and has scattered them
among his published poems in the hope that they might 'take the eye'

of Jemima! De Vane describes this as being 'one of the clearest and simplest of Browning's lyrics'. I wish he had given a simple explanation of the revival of the name Pauline – the name of the poem which was too intimate for him to publish openly and which caused him life-long embarrassment.

Robert wrote *Porphyria's Lover* in which a man strangles his best-beloved to hold forever a love which he knows would have been fleeting. My father when reciting this poem said that the poet when writing it had felt poignantly a love which he was unable to consummate for social reasons, and that he came to terms with the problem by working it out in his poetry. In this poem he saw the solution of strangling it in his mind to hold on forever to the last blissful emotion – in suspended animation, like the Perseus and Andromeda picture.

In *Evelyn Hope* the poet is consoled by the thought that when one is unable to fulfil a love in this life, there will be an opportunity in a future life:

> I claim you still, for my own love's sake!
> Delayed it may be for more lives yet,
> Through worlds I shall traverse not a few –
> Much is to learn and much to forget
> Ere the time be come for taking you.
> But the time will come, – ...

For his problem, Robert thought travelling might be a remedy. Uncle Reuben thought so too. With the connivance of William Shergold in Paris, he was able to negotiate a trip on behalf of Rothschild to St. Petersburg, by a round-about route, for about three months, early in 1834, some two years after *Pauline* was written. (Who will ever know now how many detailed poems were written meanwhile, which were destroyed?) Browning corresponded with his family while he was away on this most interesting journey, but as John Maynard says, 'Browning destroyed the letters he wrote home to his family'. I was told that Reuben and Robert would never have referred to their Rosicrucian secrets on paper, so what other cause would there be to destroy letters to Reuben and to Jemima and home, if they were not filled with emotional problems, yearnings or personal sentiments which would arouse suspicion and cause gossip among the rest of the family? Surely descriptions of what he saw on his voyage, such as appear in *Iv*à*n Iv*à*novitch* need not be destroyed? Indeed they would have been useful for reference.

Robert began his poem *Paracelsus* at this time. He wrote the poem after his return, stating that it had been thought of but six months previously, which means he probably had reason to anticipate it prior to his journey abroad.

De Vane found amusing Browning's own postscript on *Paracelsus* – 'The liberties I have taken with my subject are very trifling and the reader may slip the foregoing scenes between the leaves of any memoir of Paracelsus he pleases, by way of commentary.' A nonchalant 'throwaway' remark if ever there was one, to hoodwink readers into ignoring the deeply autobiographical implications throughout the poem!

I have already mentioned a reason for why I believe Festus to represent Reuben. I now refer to Michal's representation of Jemima. Paracelsus leaves Michal who represents woman's love (in the poem as wife of Festus) only to find problems in the path he chooses as he sacrifices love. Michal is dead by the end of the poem, and I believe Robert went away on this journey to eradicate the thought of personal love for Jemima – hoping the thought would be dead on his return.

Paracelsus expresses the view, as Robert no doubt did before his departure:

> My own affections laid to rest awhile,
> Will waken purified ...
>
>   ... I am saved
> The sad review of an ambitious youth
> Choked by vile lusts, unnoticed in their birth
> But let grow up and around a will
> Till action was destroyed.

and he has Festus say what Reuben might well have said of Jemima:

> O very proud will Michal be of you!
> Imagine how we sat, long winter-nights ...
> ... it was strange how, even when most secure
> In our domestic peace, a certain dim
> And flitting shade could sadden all; it seemed
> A restlessness of heart, a silent yearning,
> A sense of something wanting, incomplete –
> Not to be put in words.

Rosicrucian training helped Robert more than his mother's religion to fight against what he knew to be wrong, as he explored the realms of the spirit more and more, to overcome the problems which existed until 1845 when the time was right for him to find Elizabeth. As for Jemima, if he loved her company before he went away, he loved her just as much, if not more, when he came back, even if the break had given him the courage to fight any illicit passion. He threw himself into work in the theatre, and in 1838 went on his first visit to Italy to search for material for another poem, *Sordello*. When he returned his immediate family and half-family were neighbours with Reuben's horse York stabled in his own stables. By this time the rest of the nine children had departed. William Shergold was married and living in Paris. Jane, who had been jealous of Jemima's exclusive friendship with the poet, had married a John Mason (whose son Cyrus later left a memoir of the family); Christiana had died, Mary had married, and Louisa and Sarah had left to establish a nearby school. Thomas had been sent away, which left only Reuben and Jemima at home, with Reuben busy at work with the House of Rothschild.

I believe Robert and Jemima made a heroic and constant effort to become absorbed with everything and everybody other than each other. While Robert busied himself in the theatre Jemima helped out in the school of which her two sisters were principals in Dartmouth Row, Blackheath; but there were inevitably the times when they were alone at home together when it would have been pointless not to run through the fields, laugh and talk, ride together as they had always done. They were so happy in each other's company.

I think each showed indifference at times, and interest in the opposite sex, when reason prevailed and showed that the only answer to their problem lay in fulfilled marriage to someone else since they could never marry each other.

To me the basis of all the poet's allusions to non-consummation of love is the emotional conflict in the years when Robert and Jemima were in close proximity, in the six or seven years prior to Robert's courtship of Elizabeth. The *Statue and the Bust* depicts the waste of passion as years pass and the lady looks from the window of the room where she is imprisoned, to where the object of her love, the Arch-Duke Ferdinand, rides by, and each of them postpones the fulfilment of their love until their youth and looks have gone away and they immortalise the situation by placing a bust of the lady in the window to look down on the square where the Arch-Duke had a statue erected of himself so that the statue and bust looked at each other in an emotional 'impasse'. Robert and Jemima were not to become a Statue and a Bust!

In a small poem *Cristina* based on a situation involving the Queen of Sweden, Browning again writes of the frustation of the fruitless love, and as Phelps points out,* 'In *Cristina*, the man's love is not rewarded here, he fails; ... He will always love her – in losing her he has found a guiding principle for his own life, which will lead him ever up and on.'

A favourite poem of many is *The Last Ride Together*, which Edward Berdoe considered the greatest. It used to bring tears to my eyes when my father recited it after explaining that there really was a last ride when Robert was unable to marry someone he loved. He expressed the philosophical opinion in the poem that perhaps it would not have worked out had they married, and that a solution would be for him to go abroad permanently:

> ... it seemed my spirits flew,
> Saw other regions, cities new.

and, ever the optimist, Browning finds consolation in

> The instant made eternity, –
> And heaven just prove that I and she
> Ride, ride together, forever ride?

The courage of acceptance of the unrequited love and the determination to sublimate it is to be praised, but how much more praiseworthy is it when one knows that in real life the poet had to enact this very situation!

In 1842 Robert began a new long poem, a romance called *The Flight of the Duchess*, a story said to have been inspired by a gypsy song he heard when a child – he must have heard several about joining the raggle-taggle gypsies-o, and following the Queen of the gypsies-o. The whole is a complicated story which, if simplified, describes how a young woman, tied to a formal, loveless relationship with the Duke, is transformed by magic as the gypsy tells of the power of real love. 'She was telling her how good a thing is love – how strong and beautiful the double existence of those whom love has welded together,' says Mrs. Sutherland Orr, who then comes to the conclusion that 'the poetic truth of the Duchess's romance is incompatible with rational explanation'.

* *Browning*, Murray 1915.

To me it is clearly the selfless working out of Robert's problem. He always did see in the passionate gypsies a lovely full-blooded un-inhibited expression of their love – a love which would be denied to Jemima in their own relationship. In telling the story of the expression on the face of the Duchess when she learns of the ecstasy of uninhibited love, I am sure he was unselfishly convincing himelf of the rationality of welcoming Jemima's love affair with another man, in the fulfilment of marriage. This would be the very opposite of the irrationality Mrs. Sutherland Orr attributed to her friend.

This poem was started two years before Robert set off on a second more leisurely journey to Italy in the summer of 1844, when he was thirty-two and Jemima thirty-three. During his absence she had become betrothed to William Hixon.

When Robert returned home in December 1844 he had no-one on whom to pour the torrent of love in his heart. On January 10, 1845, Robert Browning wrote to the famous poetess of Wimpole Street, whom he had never met, 'I love your verses with all my heart, dear Miss Barrett ... I do, as I say, love these books with all my heart – and I love you too.'* Later in the year Jemima married William Hixon. Robert attended the ceremony and 'Kissed the chancel steps where she had been standing.'†

Although the poet destroyed all material evidence of any associa-tion with Jemima, the facts are that he thought her beautiful, remained unattached as long as she was living near him to be his 'constant com-panion', and that his first poem *Pauline* and subsequent poems of un-requited love have not otherwise been explained. Moreover there is a family tradition, repeated by Jemima's own granddaughter, that the poet loved her. References, made decades later, to the period spent with Jemima appear to support the story. In *Letters of Robert Browning* edited by T. L. Hood there appears on March 4, 1887, a letter to Furni-vall referring to 'The Song of David' as a basis for *Saul*. He writes, 'after nearly fifty years, I remember the whole pretty well ... on an occasion that would excuse much mistiness in my memory.' De Vane writes, 'The occasion was probably his first acquaintance with Miss Barrett,' – but simple arithmetic makes it nearly eight years before Elizabeth, and in the Jemima period.

Similarly, concerning *The Flight of the Duchess*, De Vane writes, 'in the part of the poem written in the spring and summer of 1845, it is quite clear that in Browning's mind Miss Barrett took the place

* *The Browning Love Letters*, Murray 1899.
† Talking of the Brownings, *Browning Society Notes*, Vol. 3 No. 3, Dec. 1973.

of the duchess, and that he used the poem as a part of his courtship'. De Vane is perceptive and correct in his statement, but the possibility of the obvious inspiration of someone else, since the poem was started in 1842, is overlooked. De Vane could not guess that it could be the poet's solution for his problem with Jemima.

My grandmother, who was living in Sydney at the time, sent us a copy of John Scarlett's article in *The Sydney Morning Herald* of September 27, 1937, as soon as she saw it, and had comments to make on Cyrus Mason's memory of an incident – a farewell between the step-grandmother and the poet: 'As she sat in her chair one morning the door was thrown open, and Browning ran to her side, his face alight with excitement. Taking his startled grandmother's hands in his own, he exclaimed: "A monstrous mistake! According to the Book of Common Prayer, a man is forbidden to marry his grandmother – the pity of it!"' My grandmother wondered whether the young lad Cyrus, who was a visitor in the house at the time, might not have remembered this as part of a discussion about other relations mentioned in the prayer book who are precluded from holy wedlock!

In *The Ring and the Book*, Browning's poem in twelve books of a true seventeenth-century murder story, a child-bride Pompilia is rescued from her wicked husband Guido Franceschini by a priest Caponsacchi, and they flee to Rome to her parents so that her baby may be born in a peaceful atmosphere. The husband arranged for them to be pursued by murderers. Pompilia's parents are slain when the door is opened to the murderers and Pompilia is mortally wounded, but able to give a dying testament. It is the story of the love between Pompilia and the priest Caponsacchi in which Browning comes into his own. He gives witness to their Platonic relationship, to the fact that even though they have lain together in love for each other, that love was divine – there was no sin to blemish its purity. Pompilia tells how she –

> ... found Caponsacchi and escaped.
> And this man, men call sinner? Jesus Christ!
> Of whom men said, with mouths Thyself mad'st once,
> 'He hath a devil' – say he was Thy saint...

The saving of Pompilia from a harsh domestic atmosphere would have revived memories of Robert's elopement with Elizabeth from Wimpole street, but I believe the situation of the non-consummated love is based on all his memories of life with Jemima which could equally have been tainted unjustifiably by gossips. Pompilia reminds us of her beloved:

> ...He is a priest;
> He cannot marry therefore, which is right:...
> In heaven we have the real and true and sure ...
> Be as the angels rather, who, apart
> Know themselves into one, are found at length
> Married, but marry never ...
> ... they are man and wife at once
> When the true time is ...

To support my suggestion that Robert was thinking back to his situation with Jemima with whom he used to play when her mother visited, through Pompilia he remembers:

> She brought a neighbour's child of my own age
> To play with me of rainy afternoons;
> And, since there hung a tapestry on the wall,
> We two agreed to find each other out
> Among the figures ...
> You know the figures never were ourselves
> Though we nick-named them so. Thus, all my life ...
> I touch a fairy thing that fades and fades.

He and Jemima shared conversations many times, playing at make-believe in front of the picture of Perseus and Andromeda, the picture which was with him in reality or imagination all his life.

Robert's love for Elizabeth was destined to be the perfect love. In telling the family story of Robert's affection for his aunt, I want to emphasise my belief that it was his heroic coping with the situation which stretched his capacity for loving, so that by the time he was united with his true love, he was able to give Elizabeth the especially strong and powerful love which she needed, to elope with him to Italy and become a fulfilled wife and mother.

When thinking about the place of this perfect love in the scheme of things, and when reading of Browning's written declaration of love in his first letter before he had even met her, I was aware of the inevitability of that love. I was overwhelmingly convinced that there was born into both Robert and Elizabeth seeds of a love which had been unable to grow and bear fruit in a past life. I believe that reincarnation is possible with a repeat of a pre-destined arrangement of inherited genes, so that I wondered if ancestors of Robert and Elizabeth respectively had fallen in love only to be torn apart. This would account for the magnetic attraction of souls, as happened with Robert and Elizabeth. Imagine my feelings when I read the research of scholars who traced back the Browning and Barrett ancestors to adjacent territory in the West Indies at the same point of time! Such a romance as I envisaged could have been possible. If the scientific exploration into reincarnation and the behaviour of genes progresses, perhaps future students will be able to support my theory in respect of Robert and Elizabeth.

3 · The Poet in Retreat

The Barretts of Wimpole Street ends with Elizabeth Barrett Moulton-Barrett's departure from home, with her maid Wilson and her dog Flush. She was secretly married to Robert at '$\frac{1}{4}$11–11$\frac{1}{4}$ a.m.', as recorded by Robert, in St. Marylebone Church, London, on Saturday, September 12, 1846. After the ceremony, she returned to 50 Wimpole Street as though nothing had happened, and Robert returned home to tell his mother and father. The elopement took place a week later, via France to Italy.

In Florence they embarked on a married life more idyllic than their wildest dreams, with Robert away from the Browning family to 'the cities new' which he had envisaged. They settled for nearly all their married life in an apartment in Casa Guidi, Piazza San Felice. Here they made many friends, Elizabeth took her first long walk, and continued to improve in health until she could travel by donkey into the countryside for picnics. Robert took care of the housekeeping. Elizabeth blossomed under the love and devotion of Robert.

Two views of the courtyard and of Casa Guidi where Flush is said to have been buried.

At Casa Guidi they lived and loved to the full, and supported each other in moments of crisis. It was at Casa Guidi that Elizabeth's beloved and faithful Flush died and was buried to be an eternal part of that harmonious household. Was ever dog so honoured? – even having a biography written by Virginia Woolf? It was at Casa Guidi in 1849 that their son Robert Barrett Browning, or Robert Wiedemann Browning, or Penini or Pen for short, was born. My grandmother wrote that his nickname came from a friend of his father. There are several other versions of how he came by his unusual name, including

ELIZABETH BARRETT BROWNING and PEN, 1860.

one that Penini was the way Pen himself pronounced Wiedemann. However he came by it, Pen he remained.

It was over their son Pen that they had one of their few disagreements, which proved they were human! Elizabeth would dress the boy, even when he grew quite big, in effeminate finery, and let his curly locks grow. Robert had to make a manly protest at the curls and lace and fripperies on the rapidly growing, precocious lad. Underneath the appearance of a 'mummy's boy in drag', there lurked a tough-thinking, sporting little tomboy, a daredevil and a future all-round sportsman of no mean prowess, but until the end Elizabeth had her way, and the fine clothes became characteristic of him. He himself liked them and saw them as no impediment to his tree-climbing, or riding horseback furiously, or playing soldiers. Robert continued vainly to protest while he endeavoured to give him the same thorough musical, linguistic and wide literary education he himself had received.

Another disagreement was over Elizabeth's active interest in spiritualism. Rosicrucian Robert was no disbeliever in life after death, or even the ability to communicate with the soul of a loved one. He was merely alarmed that his intelligent wife was taking a morbid interest in the type of séances which were popular in that day, with the accompanying table-lifting and physical phenomena which were occasionally proven to be trickery. Even if they were genuine, as he well knew could be the case, they were beneath consideration for the growth of the Divine Spirit within, which Robert privately sought.

At the time of Pen's birth, Robert's mother died and for a while he was inconsolable. Grief must be allowed to run its normal course; while this happened Robert was still the caring husband and the attentive father, seeing to the practical needs of the family. When the grief passed, the perfect contentment in their married life in Italy returned.

There appeared to be no limit to what Elizabeth was able to do, no restriction on the distances she could travel, by whatever means of transport, after the birth of Pen. They made periodical visits home to London and to Paris, for holidays with friends or to see to little family matters such as Robert's father's breach of promise suit. The seventy-year-old made a rash proposal of marriage to a much younger widow Müller, and when he wished to retract she sued him. Robert arrived in London, with family, after the trial but in time to place his father out of harm's way in Paris, with his sister Sarianna to look after him there. This was in 1852.

As the years passed Elizabeth was threatened by bouts of her old illness and she returned to the use of her morphine medicine. In 1861

ELIZABETH BARRETT BROWNING; taken in Rome, 1860.

her health rapidly declined and on June 29, she died in love and happiness, without pain, in Robert's arms in their bedroom with the white doves on the ceiling. It can be seen still today in their Casa Guidi apartment with the narrow balcony facing the church of San Felice, whose plaintive-toned bell still tolls the passing hours. Robert's ambition had been fulfilled in giving her a healthy, active life and motherhood. In death she looked young and well.

Belonging to this period of life at Casa Guidi, before the death of

Elizabeth, is an old and beautifully embossed portfolio.* My father kept a magical compendium of significant Rosicrucian symbols and was sure that the poet must have done the same. My grandmother said that he frequently referred to these in communicating with Reuben, but he destroyed everything which might lead people to suspect he was more than the ordinarily knowledgeable human being that he was. Among my family papers is the reproduction of part of just such a compendium, and a copy of *The American University Courier*, Vol. XXIV No. 3 of April 1918, which reports that the portfolio was given by Fannie Barrett Browning to Samuel J. MacWatters, who gives details of a sketch drawn by the poet, while living at Casa Guidi.

'The figure of the locust, with the face of a man and the crown upon its head (see Revelation 9:7, "On their heads were as it were crowns like gold, and their faces were as the faces of men"), resting upon a globe, was drawn by the hand of the poet. After Mrs. Browning passed from earth, Mr. Browning reversed the portfolio ... and on the opposite page placed the re-print of his wife's poem, *How do I love thee?*

As though in response to the sonnet Robert Browning had penned the previously unpublished poem:

SHE SHALL SPEAK TO ME

She shall speak to me in places lone,
With a low and holy tone.
Ay! When I have lit my lamp at night,
She shall be present with my sprite;
And I will say, whate'er it be,
Every word she telleth me.

The Hebrew, Latin and Italian lines accompanying the stanza, and the Greek and Hebrew inscriptions beneath and near the figure shown above it, furnish the students of Browning new and interesting problems of interpretation ...

Translations, with Notes
Hebrew, above the stanza: 'The possession eternal.'
Latin, below the stanza, from Vergil, Aenid, 4, 83:

'Absent (she) both hears and sees (him) absent.'

* Now in Armstrong Browning Library, Waco, Texas.

This sentence was used by Browning in 1887 in the dedication of his book, *Parleyings with Certain People of Importance in Their Day*, to the memory of ... J. Milsand, who had died the previous year. ...

Italian, below the Latin: 'For the day.'

Hebrew, obliquely above and to the right of the figure:

'To the place.'

Greek, below the figure, from Euripides, *Medea*, 410:

'Upstream the headwaters of the sacred rivers flow.'

This sentence is the first line of the first strophe of one of the choruses of the drama, introducing a passage presaging a sea-change in the attitude of the world towards woman. ...

Every literary and symbolic feature of the portfolio is an invitation, nay, more, a challenge to their best endeavour at interpretation by those who have been most successful in following the flight of Browning's singing soul through the moral and spiritual universe of his published poetry. Who accepts?'

As this was sixty years ago, I should not be surprised that my repeated letters trying to find the whereabouts of the portfolio today bore no results, but by one of the many 'roots of coincidence' I have with Browning, I had a picture postcard this year from my daughter Yolanda who was teaching in Florence, bearing a symbol which sent me scuttling for my family paper. I was startled at the similarity.

Left: Symbol drawn by Robert Browning in a private compendium, during his stay in Florence, 1847–1861.

Right: Picture postcard of a carnival celebration in Florence, 1978.

Browning must have seen a similar symbolic figure in a Florentine procession well over a hundred years ago, and my daughter sent me a card to say that she had seen it – the face was supposed to be that of the president and the festival was something to do with fertility, and phallic symbols, giant-sized, were used playfully to tap people on the head!

Browning has put a cross on the ball – I wonder was it a rosy cross? He has put angels wings on the 'sprite' – to make it represent Elizabeth? 'O Lyric Love, half-angel and half-bird' ... Was it a fertility symbol for her?

She was buried in Florence, and Robert was to harbour another emotional experience in suspended animation until he could join his beloved in spirit. He took his young son to England, vowing never to return to Florence where his heart lay buried. He returned to London, to the headquarters of that much-changed, greatly increased Browning family, most of whom meant nothing to him, but about whom he was fed constant news which he was courteous enough to acknowledge.

Pen's story, amply illustrated, is told by Maisie Ward in *The Tragi-Comedy of Pen Browning* (Sheed & Ward and The Browning Institute, 1972). He married a wealthy American, Fannie Coddington, in 1887 when he was thirty-eight and she five years younger. They had met many years earlier. They lived in the Palazzo Rezzonico, Venice, where Pen designed a shrine to his mother. Here Robert Browning died in 1889, tended by Fannie, who described the last hours in *Some Memoirs of Robert Browning* (Boston: Marshall Jones Company, 1928). The marriage broke up two years later, I believe because Fannie was not adapted to married life, especially with an artist who painted and modelled nudes, as she was extremely prudish. She had miscarriages which must have left her emotionally disturbed, and would account for her tantrums. She liked female companionship and was devoted to her sister Marie with whom she corresponded daily if Marie was separated from her, otherwise Marie lived in the marital home.

Fannie was known to have taken in a blonde model Ginevra as nurse-companion and permanent member of the household. When Pen and Fannie quarrelled and she left home for medical treatment, leaving Ginevra in charge, malicious gossip made poor Ginevra the scapegoat for the lack of domestic bliss. When Fannie received sympathy from gossips who raised eyebrows because Pen had been left with the lovely blonde girl, she said nothing in his defence, or to lessen the compassion of friends, from which she drew comfort.

The facts are that Ginevra was openly introduced as a member of the household, first when Fannie was there and later when Aunt Sarianna joined the household in Asolo, and Ginevra was married with Pen's blessing – all very unlikely situations to give real cause for scandal. Gossip there was, until Pen, usually silent on such matters, was driven to state that it was inconceivable that he should ever consider taking a mistress into his marital home with his wife still present.

FANNIE CODDINGTON 1854?–1935

Fannie eventually settled in England at Anchorhold, Haywards Heath. Her last companion there was Miss Maud Ivatt who asked me to visit her alone on two occasions. She was receiving heavy doses of cortisone for crippling arthritis, but she was anxious to talk about Fannie.

She asked if I knew that Ginevra was Pen's daughter! She said that Fannie was extremely fond of Ginevra, and would dearly have loved her to be her own daughter. She adored the poet but was constantly being shocked by Pen, with his nudes and his domestic pets, and the strain of living in that household, when she knew finally that

MISS MAUD IVATT, Fannie's companion.

she could not give Pen a child, was too much. She was happier being the famous poet's daughter-in-law and the beneficent donor of Browningiana to open-handed Browning-lovers.

Maud Ivatt left me Fannie's photographs. On the back of two photographs of herself embracing Pen were pictures of a beautiful blonde girl and a baby unnamed. Ginevra had a son whom Maisie Ward mentions having met when on a visit to Asolo.

Fannie devoted herself to good works, regularly donating money to a local religious order, and she founded the Robert Browning Settlement 'A World Memorial to a World Poet', at Browning Hall,

Walworth, the premises where Robert and his sister Sarianna had been baptized. I have in front of me a 1928 poster of the Settlement with a photograph of the Patron 'Mrs Robert Barrett Browning', and 'Our President and Mrs. Mather – Golden Wedding Photo', and some eighty activities advertised, from Fairies, through Stamp Collectors and Christmas Goose Club to Grandmother's Club. They retain many interesting Browning items today, including a bust of the poet sculptured by his son. This gesture was Fannie's tribute to the poet.

Pen's tribute was to be Casa Guidi, his birthplace and his beloved home during his mother's lifetime, but when he died in 1912 he was buried in the Protestant cemetery in Florence after being moved from Asolo and all the Browning items were sold at a massive Sotheby's sale in 1913, the proceeds being divided among sixteen Barrett cousins. What looked like disaster ten years ago when Casa Guidi was threatened with demolition looks hopeful today. Philip Kelley, as President of the New York Browning Society, raised the money to secure the Browning apartment, and formed the Browning Institute with Dr. Peter Heydon as President to restore and run Casa Guidi as an attractive Browning Museum and Library. It is hoped to restore the salon and the bedroom as they were when the Brownings were in residence, as a tourist attraction to be opened officially in June 1979. This will be the European Browning Centre, which has the support of the Armstrong Browning Library while they continue to enlarge their own unique Browning collection in Waco.

The Browning Society of London was revived, with the help of descendants of both Browning and Barrett families as well as of dedicated Browning-lovers, to facilitate the study of the works of both Browning poets and also, registered as a charity, to collect donations to help restore and preserve the Casa Guidi apartment.

5 · The Browning Family which Grew and Scattered (1) William Shergold Browning, (2) Jane Eliza Browning, (3) Jemima, (4) Mary, Louisa and Sarah Anne, (5) Reuben and his children

1. WILLIAM SHERGOLD BROWNING

William Shergold Browning was the reliable, friendly uncle who married, while Robert was very young, Louisa Mansir, whose brother Robert married Mary, William Shergold's sister. In 1824, after working in the Bank of England, he took his family to Paris where he worked in a branch of the House of Rothschild for about twenty-three years. While there he provided a holiday home and exciting social life for numerous relatives in the capital of France, where most Browning young ladies attended a Finishing School attached to a convent for at least some time during their 'teens.

In true Browning tradition William Shergold adapted enthusiastically to his work and to a productive life apart from it. He devoted time to scholarship, religion, literature and the arts. He wrote several books, including *Hoel Morvan: or the Court and Camp of Henry V*, and the *History of the Huguenots* which went into several editions and was translated into German. He also contributed to the *Gentleman's Magazine* and *Leisure Hours*.

They had ten children. The eldest surviving son was born in 1824, named Robert Shergold. He lived to work in Hinckley Bank and to marry Harriet Caldecott Triquet, the daughter of a Browning colleague in the Bank of England, W. D. Triquet. They in turn had several children, the eldest being Robert Jardine Browning, born in 1853 while the poet was in Italy. He graduated as an M.A. at Lincoln College, Oxford, and went to Australia to live and become Crown Prosecutor of New South Wales. He wrote *Municipalities Acts*, thus carrying on the Browning tradition. Although prominent in his own right he felt pride in being related to the famous English poet and kept in touch with him and other relatives, especially those coming to Australia.

Another son of Robert Shergold, Charles Dearmer, married a

cousin Maud, daughter of Robert Shergold's sister Christiana who married a T. Carr.

Another son, Arthur, took Holy Orders and as the Rev. Arthur

ROBERT SHERGOLD BROWNING (4 on Family Tree B)
Born December 13, 1824. Married Harriet Caldecott Triquet, daughter of W. D. Triquet, of the Bank of England.
Children – four boys and one girl:
ROBERT JARDINE BROWNING (11 on family tree) born 1853.
M.A. Lincoln College, Oxford. Became Crown Prosecutor of New South Wales, Sydney, knew Reuben's children personally.
Married Beatrice L. Lamb of Sydney.
HARRIET ELIZABETH born 1854. Married J. F. Firth Jnr. Had two daughters, three sons. (12)
PERCY BROWNING born 1856. Father of Percy Triquet Browning – (13, 14)
CHARLES DEARMER BROWNING born 1859. Solicitor. Married his first cousin Louisa Maud Carr (15). Died 1913.
ARTHUR BROWNING Rev. Arthur Browning mentioned in David Niven's autobiography. Born 1867. Became Rector of Pangbourne, Berks (16)
Taken August 6, 1888 *left to right* (back row) ROBERT JARDINE   ARTHUR
    CHARLES DEARMER
left to right (middle row) LOUISE MAUD   HARRIET (TRIQUET)   ROBERT
SHERGOLD   CHRISTIANA MARY   EDWARD HINGSTON(?)   GERTRUDE
HINGSTON(?)

Browning, in his old age took in as paying guests young students whom he coached. The actor David Niven was one such student of mathematics and remembers the Rev. Arthur as 'magnificent-looking' with 'clear, blue eyes and white, wavy hair' (*The Moon is a Balloon*). The late Robert Calverley of the New Barnet Literary and Debating Society told a Browning Society meeting of the days spent in the Rev. Arthur's Vicarage as another paying guest student. He described the family as being very lively and full of character. The place had plenty of books for reference and the Rev. Arthur produced quotations from them.

William Shergold's eldest daughter was Elizabeth Ann Browning who married Mr. B. Sly. She was known as Aunt Bessie and towards the end of her life stayed for a time with Jemima's family, financed by the Rothschilds. News of her in family letters showed that she was in a delicate state of mental and physical health at the end of her days. Two of her sisters, Emily Frances and Ellen Jane, although not the same age, being separated by two children chronologically, were as

EMILY FRANCES and ELLEN JANE BROWNING
Emily Frances and Ellen Jane (6 and 9 on Family Tree B) were sisters, daughters of William Shergold Browning and sisters of Robert Shergold Browning.
They were so devoted to each other, as inseparable as identical twins although Emily was older then Ellen, that they were known as The Sardines. On March 12 the poet's aunt Sarah comments that Ellen felt Emily's death, so Ellen must have survived her elder sister. They lived together and looked after Mrs. Sly for a time. They gave music lessons to Norah Collings, Jemima Browning's granddaughter.

devoted and inseparable as identical twins, thus being known as the
'Sardines'. They remained unmarried, lived together, taught the
piano, and were so close in life that I have not the heart even to place
their photographs apart!

These are the few of many William Shergold descendants, whose
names and conditions would have been known to the poet at some time
in his life.

2. JANE ELIZA BROWNING

Remember the poet's Aunt Jane? She left home to marry while the
poet was young and suffered jealousy at the family attention given to
Robert and Jemima. She was continuously disagreeable and was
referred to by the family in letters as being 'as obstinate as ever' or
something equally derogatory. She left items which showed that whatever her outward appearance, she liked genteel and delicate personal
belongings – a small shopping list composed of fine ivory leaves with
minute silver pencil attached and monogrammed J.E.M. in silver, a
miniature Lexicon initialled by herself (1820), lace fans, wrought-
metal posy holders and a travelling-companion in rosewood with a
mother-of-pearl lock, its contents consisting of beauty preparations,
mother-of-pearl cotton-reels, delicate silver button-hooks, a writing
compendium with a leather-covered lid and a secret drawer for jewellery. The silver-marks were not English hall-marks but South African
silver marks of the mid-nineteenth century. I always believed she had
travelled with her family, but I cannot recall details.

Jane had married John Mason, who was traditionally son of a
widow Mason. The widow Mason was said to have married Thomas
Browning, son of William, Grandpa Browning's younger brother who
died by drowning as a young man (Furnivall's *Browning Ancestors*).
Added to the tradition of a Browning-Mason feud is the mystery that
this information is false! John Maynard's examination of Jane Mason's
son's manuscript on Robert Browning's *Kinsfolk* (Armstrong Browning Library) shows widow Mason to have married, not William's son
Thomas, but Grandpa's brother Reuben, great-great uncle to the poet.
This Reuben was said to have educated the poet's father, just as Uncle
Reuben educated the poet, making two generations of Uncle Reubens
educating nephew Roberts. It is known that this great-uncle Reuben
joined the Brownings of Camberwell in 1790 and worked in the Bank
of England for nearly thirty years. John Maynard provides in *Brown-*

ing's Youth the information that the poet's father and great-uncle Reuben and also the Masons were all connected with the York Street Congregational Chapel where the poet's mother persuaded her family to worship. Perhaps the widow Mason enticed great-uncle Reuben in the way that the poet's mother enticed her family to become members of her Chapel. Because the rest of the family attended the Church of England, John Maynard suggests that the hostility between the two sets of people may have been caused by their two differing religious denominations. The Hermetic tradition or Rosicrucian way of life should not in any way have deterred attendance at *either* religious establishment but these facts may have meant that the Masons were guilty of some breach of oath or integrity among the Rosicrucian fraternity which would account for a schism. I was always puzzled when my grandmother uttered the word 'Mason' as though it were an infectious disease and the germs in close proximity to her nose, when at the same time she offered hospitality to members of the Mason family. From this I decided the feud belonged to the era of the two Masons marrying two Brownings, that it had something to do with the poet and Cyrus Mason being enemies and ended there, and the sinister inflection when mouthing the word 'Mason' was merely as a token of respect for our poet!

John and Jane Mason had eight children, of whom Cyrus has hitherto been the most famous for his controversial manuscript *The Poet Robert Browning and his Kinsfolk*, written in his old age when he had not seen the poet since his extreme youth; he had lived all his life in Australia since that time except for a visit to his Aunts Sarah and Louise in 1900. Mistakes have been noted in his accounts. For all that, Cyrus Mason was a relative to be proud of! He was said by his own family to have resembled the poet in appearance, but from photographs, stories of his characteristics and his numerous talents he would appear to resemble more the poet's father, with a similar 'chip on the shoulder' or emotional sense of grievance, an ability to sketch with a 'cartoon' sense of humour and originality. He made naive bold pretensions on behalf of the Browning family, at the same time giving a completely false impression of the Masons as being the poor relations.

Cyrus Mason and his youngest brother Augustus Philip migrated when young to New Zealand and Australia. Cyrus Mason married Jessie Campbell, and according to my grandmother they had fourteen children. I had only eight on my family tree but various Mason descendants have said I have left out a 'Nan' and another child, another said that Jessie Campbell had previously married Philip Wortley

CYRUS and PHILIP MASON (3 and 7 respectively on Family Tree C)
CYRUS (seated), born 1828, was son of Jane (Browning) and John Mason.
Cyrus settled for years in Australia and had a large family; he died there
in 1915.
PHILIP, his brother, was christened Augustus Philip. Settled in New Zea-
land where his descendants still live.

Montagu by whom she had two daughters, Jane Stuart Wortley Montagu and Mary Edith Wortley Montagu. She was a young widow whom Cyrus had met on his way to Australia and soon after she married Cyrus she had twins, girls called Polly and Jenny who were killed in a bush fire. One Mason descendant thought Cyrus married the widow of the Duke of Manchester, another that of the Duke of Argyll and that there is a portrait of the latter Duke still in the possession of the family. What appears to be certain is that Cyrus Mason and his family set up house, which he called 'Woodyates' (after the Browning Dorset inn), in the Australian 'bush' in Tynong, and in the poet's life-time, in the eighties, formed a Bohemian Literary and Arts Club called the Buonarotti Club after the family name of Michel Angelo. My grandmother gave me a newspaper article from the *Melbourne Argus*, Camera Supplement, August 10, 1929, with a picture of Cyrus Mason and one daughter; it was one of the few editions containing a photograph of a group of its famous members. It gives full details of the activities of this unusual cultural club (I left my copy at the Armstrong Browning Library for reference). The club lasted only one year as a gentlemen's club and a further two years as a mixed club, but its activities during that time were prominent enough to make their mark on Australian cultural history.

There were two other sons born to Jane and John Mason, the eldest, Reuben, died in Bristol aged twenty-eight, and Arthur who died in New York.

Augustus Philip, known as Philip, married Emma Amelia Evans and two granddaughters have communicated with me recently to let me know of many members of the family still surviving in Australia and New Zealand, and of a Browning letter still in the possession of the family.

All the members of the Mason family were lively and adventurous, the girls as much as, if not more than, the boys. Two of the daughters, Eliza Jane and Sarianna, married two brothers Edwin and William Goodwin. They were builder and architect and lived in Ferryside, South Wales, where members of the Browning family visited frequently. Later Sarianna's husband William Goodwin built a large house he designed for her, in the Croydon area, near the home of Uncle Reuben. Eliza Jane was delicate in health and had no children. Sarianna from all accounts was a 'poppet' and inspired a great-niece to write this account:

'I loved being with Aunt Sanna – she was not tall ... cheerful as a bird always, in spite of Uncle William her husband who looked

ELIZA JANE MASON (*left*)
Daughter of Jane and John Mason, and sister of Sarianna and Cyrus.
She married Ed. Goodwin, brother of William who married Sarianna.
Lived in Ferryside, South Wales, where this picture of her in Welsh costume
was taken.

SARIANNA MASON (*right*)
Married William Goodwin. The Goodwin brothers were architects and
builders.

exactly like Bernard Shaw, was an atheist and a vegetarian. I was only
nineteen then but I had an argument with him – once when we were
walking down the main street of Croydon he said, "You know, Elaine,
Carlyle said that ninety-nine men out of a hundred are fools." I said:
"Then Carlyle must have been one of the ninety-nine!"

'He stopped in the middle of the pavement and positively roared
"What! Carlyle a fool?" I used to enjoy his outbursts;... Little Aunt
Sanna was a pet – when dusting her home she always wore a white mob
cap. I'd go marketing with her – there were nearly always "doll's cab-
bages" – Brussels sprouts – on her list.

'One memorable day she asked me if I would like to go to London
with her to see the Tower of London. We went up by an early train,
got out at Tower Bridge station and went to the Tower, only to be
told by a Beefeater that the Tower was not open to the public because
the suffragettes had threatened to damage what they could. Little Aunt
Sanna, with blue eyes and pink cheeks, and wearing a black bonnet
with peach coloured velvet bow on it, looked up at the tall Beefeater
and said, "Is it impossible? My great-niece has come all the way from

South Africa to see the Tower."

' "It's not impossible, Madam, I'll speak to the Sergeant." Back he came, with the Sergeant and another Beefeater.

' "Madam, I've told Jones to take you wherever you want to go – he has a son out in South Africa," said the Sergeant. I was so thrilled – he took us everywhere, even to parts of the Tower not usually open to the public. Being an ardent Stuart fan I looked with reverence at the block, and the axe which had taken Charles's life.'

Sarianna's daughter Kate was to become my step-grandmother when my mother was widowed and she married Kate's son Ivan Hamilton Parks.

I first saw Kate Hamilton Parks as 'Aunt Kate' in Australia when she called at our home in Melbourne during one of her round-the-world trips.

My father brought us to England in 1930 and we were soon visiting Aunt Kate regularly, the most important visits being our Boxing Day parties when we invariably had 'high' pheasant for lunch, which I cared for no more than the inevitable game of bridge which followed. I was not much more than eight years of age at the time and I feared her displeasure at my less than expert play, when she would 'Tut-tut!'

(*left*) SARIANNA and WILLIAM GOODWIN and Jumbo their cat.

(*right*) A Browning relative, probably Julia Frances Mason who married Augustus Hampden Smithers.

KATE HAMILTON-PARKS 1863–1961 (8 on Family Tree C)
Kate Hamilton-Parks daughter of Sarianna and William Goodwin, with her
husband Herbert Hamilton-Parks and elder son Frank and younger son Ivan
(9 on Family Tree C) – my step-father for thirty years. The family travelled
extensively; Kate in her widowhood sailed round the world at least three
times and lived for long spells in Australia, Africa and Canada, bearing
family news. She stayed with cousins in Africa during the Boer war and
was at finishing school in a convent in Paris with my grandmother Elizabeth.
Told many tales of their escapades and elegant living.
left to right KATE (Goodwin)   HERBERT HAMILTON-PARKS   FRANK
PARKS   IVAN

and rap the table smartly with the crisply-uttered reminder to play 'through the strength and up to the weak!' Her home was filled with the prizes she had brought back regularly from the Conservative Bridge Club for years.

When my father died in 1938 we heard that Aunt Kate's younger son Ivan had been widowed and that he was bringing his youngest two children, twin girls, to England. They stayed in our house as there was ample room. In 1940, while we children were evacuated from London with our schools, Ivan, an aircraft inspector and air raid warden, married my mother who was engaged in Red Cross nursing at the Belgrave Hospital for Children.

When our home was bombed my mother and stepfather stayed with Aunt Kate, whom I now called Gran, and Ivan's brother Frank, in Wembley. Gran wrote to me when I was an evacuee in Llanelli and told me about the large family home at 'Ferryside' where various members of the Brownings stayed in Queen Victoria's reign, and when I responded with interest she looked forward to my visits when she would talk non-stop about the 'good old days', the Mason-Browning bickering, the poet's father's breach-of-promise case, and she confirmed many of the stories of my grandmother and cousins, of the 'finishing' of Victorian young ladies in Paris, Switzerland or Germany, their lessons in deportment and the courtesies of 'calling' and introduction and general behaviour of the times.

She shared the family sense of fun and practical jokes. A Browning never expected anyone else to do anything for one that one would not be prepared to do for one's self. The poet had remarked that he would enjoy being the groom of my great-grandfather's horse York as much as the rider, which rash statement earned him the position of both! Gran applied this rule to her domestic servants too! My favourite story was of an Irish Catholic scullery-maid, who was very devout, and whose work was to scrub the wooden basement floor with soap until it was gleaming white, but the floor became increasingly grubby. The maid insisted she had indeed scrubbed it to the best of her ability and that it could look no whiter. Gran said that the good Lord would know if she were telling the truth. That night the maid went out with her young man, and Gran went to work on the floor! When our devout young Irish maid returned home at eleven and entered the basement, which was in darkness except for the light from a lamp in the street, she let out a blood-curdling scream and oaths to the Virgin Mary, for there shone out from the grimy floor a large pure white gleaming cross! Gran's magic worked, for the next day and thereafter the floor was scrubbed uniformly white without any more urging!

As a girl, Gran went visiting cousins in South Africa, next door to a military parade ground. When she and her cousin were up a tree overlooking the parade-ground but hidden in the branches, they watched the soldiers being drilled. On the command of 'As you WERE!' little Kate with a huge voice bellowed, 'Before you WAS!' and had the whole platoon in an uproar. She was not permitted to repeat her unseemly behaviour.

For her ninetieth birthday an article published in the *Wembley News* on March 26, 1953, included the following:

'Remembering Wembley Triangle when it was a mere grassy patch, she says she used to run across there to catch the horse trams to Sudbury. Her keen memory also conjures for her recollections of Queen Victoria's diamond jubilee celebrations and also of her funeral.

'Every continent in the world has been visited by Mrs. Hamilton Parks during her life. Twice she travelled round the world by herself ... She was equally at home on Canadian prairies, Australian bush land, South Sea islands or the humid jungle country of Ceylon which she visited three times.'

It was from Gran that I received the miniature photograph portrait of Jane and small mementos to preserve her memory. (The portrait is now in the Armstrong Browning Library.)

Jane Mason's youngest daughter Julia Frances was known as Fanny and married Augustus Hampden Smithers, a Freeman of the City of London with whom she sailed to South Africa in 1867 with their family. A granddaughter remembered from her grandfather's diary:

'According to it Augustus Hampden Smithers first met Julia Frances in Brussels, where he held a position in the Rothschild's Bank. He and a friend were sitting on a bench in some park in Brussels one Sunday, when coming down one of the paths he saw three people. He said to his friend, "I'll wager that is an English family." His friend said, "You are right, they are a Mr. and Mrs. Mason and their daughter, would you like to meet them?" Grandpa said yes and they were introduced. In his diary he mentioned Julia Frances's dress – white muslin, crinoline I think, and a leghorn bonnet trimmed with roses and tied under her chin with blue satin ribbon. They married and must have lived in Brussels, for Uncle Denny and Uncle Arthur were born there.

'No-one has ever found out what possessed Grandpa to come to South Africa. He had bought a farm at Lion's River, Natal, whilst he was in London, expecting to find an English-looking farmhouse on it, but found instead a house made "of wattle and daub". It was when they lived there that Uncle Denny wrote of his "laughing Mama". Grandpa had two houses in Pretoria, one of which he sold to Rider Haggard and was afterwards known as "Jess's Cottage".'

Mother used to speak of those early days in Pretoria ... Grandmama was called 'The Duchess', she carried herself so beautifully and was so gracious. This was before the 1881 Boer War. The house next door to them was occupied by an irascible Major who one day, when he found some of Grandma's fowls in his garden, wrung their necks and threw them over the wall into her garden. That night, my two Uncles Denny and Arthur caught his favourite donkey and painted it in red, white and blue stripes! Very angry Major but I believed that ended in a great friendship.

Mother was married in 1881 at St. Alban's Cathedral, Pretoria, to John Holder, our father, by Bishop Bousfield.

I don't know when the family left Pretoria for Kimberley, where everyone was finding diamonds, except that Grandpa, Mother and Father lived in Potchefstroom and then trekked to Kimberley with three children Elaine, Hampden and Mabel. We lived at the 'Homestead', some miles out of Kimberley, but I spent a lot of time with my beloved Grandmama, still the gracious lady she was and remained so until her death. We left Kimberley, and went to live on one of Father's farms in Bechuanaland, a lovely place, but by then there were seven children growing up and needing schooling, so we trekked to Johannesburg and stayed with Grandmama until Father found a house for us. How happy I was to be with her again. She always wore little lace caps, which Sybil made for her. I love balsams to this day because she had them in her garden, mignonette too; a pot of musk she kept on her kitchen window-sill.

When Father built a house of his own, she and Grandpapa moved up to be near us. Poor Grandmama – she tried so hard to teach me deportment, strictly taught in her girlhood, but I preferred to be the tomboy I was.

She taught me to be strictly honest in everything – 'not to sit on the edge of a chair, not to sew with a very long thread', only servant-maids did that, and always to put on my gloves before going into the street – as they were kid, the ends were usually well chewed. At the age of eleven or twelve I was sent to boarding-school in Natal, and only went home once a year – no railway to Johannesburg then – so I did not see much of Grandmama after that, but I have never lost the love and admiration for her. She could play the piano well and sing in French and Italian, and do many lovely things. I often look at her as she hangs above my head and remember my days with her. She is buried beside Uncle Sydney and Grandpapa in a plot in the old Braamfontein Cemetery, and on her headstone is inscribed 'He giveth His beloved sleep'.

As regards the Brownings, Mother told me that before they sailed for South Africa they were taken to say goodbye to Robert and Sarianna Browning [1867 at 19 Warwick Crescent, Paddington V.B.].

When Mother took Mabel, our second sister, to put her in school in England (Eastbourne), she went to see Sarianna Browning [29 De Vere Gardens V.B.], who was very frail. When she told her that she had been in Westminster Abbey that morning, the old lady said, 'The last time I was there was at dear Robert's funeral.' I wanted so much to meet her, but she died before I joined mother in September 1902. Actually Sarianna was with Pen in Asolo where she died in 1903.

The above account was mostly given by Elaine Holder. Her mother Mary Ethel Holder was the daughter of Julia Frances Mason and Augustus Hampden Smithers, and was born in Kent, England in 1859, while the poet was living in Florence. Her jotted notes give further details of their particular experiences, which provided news for family dinner-table talk and correspondence for years and were certainly very well known to the poet and my own grandmother who used to talk about the family travels.

'Came to South Africa in a sailing vessel *Actea*, Captain Packer, 1867. Left England 11 August, arrived in Durban on "back beach", now "Scotsmanpool" or South beach, 11 November, were carried there by the crew from the ship. During a calm in mid-ocean, the passengers were allowed to visit another ship, also becalmed, in rowing boats; were hurried back as soon as Captain saw clouds on the horizon, portending a storm. There were six of us in the family, Hampden, Arthur, Sydney, Ethel aged eight, Grace and Ellie. Sybil was born in Pretoria, S. Africa. Came out to a farm (bought on paper in England) said farm on North Coast of Natal, above Unhlauga Rocks. Travelled by ox-wagon from Durban, to the farm; fires had to be kept up at night to keep off the lions! Farm proved a failure. Father collected mussels and oysters and sent them for a short while to Durban. Heard of New Rush (now Kimberley, named after Lord Kimberley) and he went to see it, left the family at Lions River, Natal, where farming was tried. Mother opened a small school, which must have been difficult for her, as we did all our own work; it was here I was taught to make bread, and had my first and only fall from a horse. Spent 3 months in Pietermaritzburg in preparation for the trek to the "Diggings". I attended my first school kept by Mrs. Longhurst; for some small offence I received three cuts from the cane on my open hand, which I never forgot; from that time on Mother took command and educated us. We trekked to the diggings by ox-wagon, stuck in Vat river which was in flood, saw a swarm of foot-gangers, for the first time, crossing the river. Out-spanned at Bloemhof on the market square. Boers objected and called out a Commando to eject us.

The English Padre came to the rescue and we were allowed to remain. Conditions very bad at the Diggings, lived in tents as many others did. Camp fever (enteric) broke out. Ellie had it and Mother nursed her successfully. Dr. Starr Jameson (Dr. Jim of the famous Jameson Raid) persuaded Mother to nurse many other patients, although not trained, she used her common sense and was a great help to everyone. We trekked from here to the River Diggings (Riverton).

We were in very bad circumstances then, my brothers cut and sold wood to the residents.

In 1872 trekked to Pretoria passing White Waters Ridge which was a vast vlei (now Johannesburg and the Wieterssand). Settled in a tin shanty near a Dopper Church. Father, Arthur and Sydney trekked to Mac-a-mac, had no luck. Hampden was commandeered for Sekekuni War.

Mother played the organ at St. Alban's Church (now the Cathedral) for a farewell Service to the soldiers going to the war. We left the "tin shanty" and moved near to President Burgeres house; he was a tall lean man with red hair.

Father eventually bought a house and land (present site a jam factory); on this property was the cottage that Rider Haggard bought and immortalised by naming it "Jess Cottage", in his book called *Jess*.

We were in Pretoria during the siege of the first Boer War 1880, for three months. Arthur and I used to sing in the choir at St. Alban's. I went to Potchefstroom for three months in 1880 and met and married John Holder (of Hollins and Holder) ... travelled through Rustenburg to Potchefstroom by ox-wagon and lived there for four years, business firm went bankrupt. We trekked to Kimberley once more by ox-wagon, with a family of three children, Elaine,

Hampden and Mabel. Remained in Kimberley where Rhoda Hereward, Eric and Pearl were born. John worked on De Beers mine
and met Cecil Rhodes. Rhodes offered him a job in East Africa which
he accepted; but Rhodes, when he heard John was a married man,
refused to take him, as no married men were to be sent to that part
of the country ...'

So the adventures of the family continued but the poet Robert
Browning died on December 12, 1889, and so his knowledge of his
cousins' activities in South Africa went only this far.

There is another of Jane's children, the only one I have not
mentioned, Harriet Louise, the eldest daughter. She was born next
in line to Cyrus Mason. Like Sarianna and Fanny she had charm,
energy and an attractive personality. Her love of music led her to meet
the German composer-musician Bernhard Althaus. His father was
Fritz Althaus whom Fanny's granddaughter described as one of the
handsomest men she had ever seen when she met him in Brussels
through Augustus Hampden-Smithers. Since the latter worked for
Rothschild's Bank, perhaps the social life of Rothschild colleagues was
responsible for yet another match-making! Certainly this marriage of
music was dear to the heart of the poet! Harriet and Bernard Althaus
had three children, Fred, Basil and Harriet Louise, called 'Kitty' to
distinguish her from her mother.

Kitty was born the year after Elizabeth Barrett Browning died and

(*left*) HARRIET MASON, married Bernard Althaus.

(*right*) BERNARD ALTHAUS.

Robert came to England. Robert composed the poem *Abt Vogler* soon after this when he was sharing his musical interests with the Althaus family. He wrote a copy of *Abt Vogler* in his own hand in the autograph book of the concert pianist Miss Agnes Zimmermann with whom he corresponded, and whom he heard play several times. Adrian Cruft, Secretary of the Royal Society of Musicians, which holds this autograph book, gives the date of the poet's entry as December 23, 1870.

Basil was an accomplished violinist when he was young, and his two daughters Dorothy and Gladys played the 'cello and violin respectively. I believe Dorothy met her husband Frank Biffo of the Biffo Quintet while she was playing professionally in an orchestra.

I hope these details of Jane Mason's family put in a new light some of the statements made by Cyrus Mason that the poet shunned Jane and her family, and indeed all his other relatives.

3. JEMIMA

Jemima married William Hixon in 1845 and lived in a beautiful house in Strathmore Terrace, Kensington. They had four children. The first, Jane, married Captain Davies Smith who served in the Boer war and was later an invalid. Jane was admired by the rest of the family for her nursing of him, and for her mobility on a bicycle! The second, William, was the son and heir, through whom a large number of Browning family letters, documents, autograph books, sketch books, photograph albums and furniture were preserved. He married Ellen Hendy and they had one daughter Nora, who later married Mr. Alfred Collings. Jemima's secure family life attracted the Browning spinster invalids and unfortunates when they were in need, and this hospitality meant that their autograph books and sketch books provide examples of original sketches, poems, portraits of nearly all the contemporary members of William Shergold and Reuben families, the poet and his father and many famous friends, and the dating and subject matter confirm biographical information.

Their third child was a son Bristow, who stowed away to Australia, married Emma Boughton, and had three daughters, Clara Mabel, Nellie, and Maude, born between 1882 and 1884. Thus Robert Browning, before his death in 1889, had the satisfaction of knowing that Jemima, who died in 1880, was succeeded by grandchildren.

The fourth child born to Jemima and William Hixon was Clara who married Ralph Cassie. They in turn, had one child called Clara,

Strathmore Gardens, Kensington, the home of Jemima and William Hixon after their marriage in 1845.

The chair used by Robert Browning, grandfather of the poet, at the Bank of England.

who married William Huxham and they had one daughter Cassie.

The family heirlooms still in the possession of Jemima's grand-daughter Mrs Nora Collings include the chair used by the poet's grandfather in the Bank of England.

4. MARY, LOUISA AND SARAH ANNE

Mary was the fifth child of Robert and Jane Smith Browning. She was born in 1805, married first to Robert Mansir whose sister Louisa married William Shergold, and secondly to Dr. G. Mason, who is not known to be related to aforementioned Masons. She had only one son who died when he was a baby.

Louisa, born in 1807, was engaged twice but never married. She and Sarah the youngest, born in 1814, the same year as the poet's sister Sarianna and named after her, ran a school in Dartmouth Row, Black-heath. The school was financed by their father initially in the sum of £200 and thereafter by small gifts of money. Jemima also took an interest in teaching at the school for a while.

The two Principals of the school always lived together, first at the school and then in Haverstock Hill near Hampstead Heath, until Louisa died in 1887; Sarah lived on until 1902. I have heard from all branches of the family that routine visits to the 'Aunts' were as regular as though they were on the school curriculum. Dozens of letters from them remained in the family, full of advice on religion and morals and exchanging the wider family news all over the world rather like an International Telegraph office and Personal Advice column all rolled into one. They kept in touch with many of their 'children' from the school and regarded them as part of their own family. They used to stay with relatives in Wales until they were physically unable to make the journey. The poet knew one or other of them for the whole of his life and regarded them with admiration tinged with amusement at their undeviating discipline. My grandmother, after the death of Reuben, was regarded for a time as 'the fish who got away' since she led a secret life. Aunt Sarah and Aunt Louisa did not know what she was doing, so no-one knew, except Robert the poet, who kept her secret.

5. REUBEN AND HIS CHILDREN

After his two nearest and dearest relatives, Jemima and Robert, had

REUBEN with his wife and family (with exception of Michael – abroad?) *l to r* (1) ELIZABETH, with croquet mallet, standing (2) DOODUM, seated on grass, holding a doll, (3) MARGARET, their mother, seated next to her two youngest daughters, (4) THOMAS HENRY, seated, (5)MARGARET, seated on grass, (6) REUBEN, seated with book, (7) ROBERT REUBEN, eldest son, seated next to his father, (8) WILLIAM, standing, (9) CHRISTINA, eldest daughter, standing.

married, Reuben missed their convivial company. Shorty afterwards he met twenty-five-year-old Margaret Lewis and married her. She was the daughter of the owner of a tweed factory, in Bryncrag, about two miles outside Aberdovey, Wales. Her home was Penhelig, where she was born on Treffrue Farm. My grandmother said a man called Griffiths swindled them out of the property.

Reuben fell in love with the Welsh countryside, which he visited and painted in water-colours, and sketched whenever he could. He wanted to buy the property at Treffrue, which had a miniature castle on a rock stretching out as a headland into the river. A descendant of Margaret's brother, master mariner Lewis Lewis, wrote that later in life Reuben negotiated to buy the property but had a stroke at a crucial time and the deal fell through.

Seven of Reuben and Margaret's eight children were born while Robert was in Italy. To accommodate them, they acquired a large house, which they called 'Penhelig', in Morland Road, Shirley, Croydon, Surrey.

The children in order of birth were: *Christina*, musical and artistic

but otherwise more practical than intellectual. She composed songs
and piano music under the names of Violet Seymour, her own name
and a male pseudonym which she used to compose marching songs
for the soldiers in the Boer war. A piano composition *Almée, Danse
Egyptienne* was printed in an album called *Orange Blossoms*. A Lewis
descendant remembers a song called *Duty's Call* being sent to the
family by Christina's sister Margaret, and Jemima's granddaughter

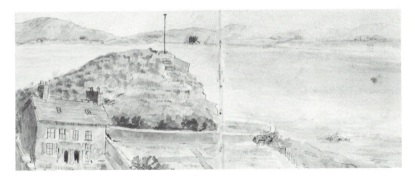

Three water-colours from a small sketchbook of Reuben Browning's,
Penhelig, Aberdovey, 1864.

had some pieces composed by Christina who stayed with her family for some time and was her godmother, giving her a lovely doll's or miniature china tea-set, which she still has, and taking her shopping.

To the poet and her immediate family she was always known as Chrissie, although she used the names Christiana and Rubina as well. She painted in oils seemingly endless pictures of fruit, which, in wooden frames, adorned most of the walls of the various relatives. She made bonnets for the ladies of the family, performed extravaganzas on the piano at the At-homes, or soirées, but in later years she felt the mental burden of being the eldest unmarried daughter. She became confused over the information which she gave about the family, substituting Shergold for Seymour and vice versa, and elaborating on the stories that the Brownings were supposed to be descended from Henry VII or VIII, and/or the Seymours of Somerset. In her insecurity she may have been trying to compensate for the fame which eluded her real talents, in establishing famous family connections. She died in her fifties about 1895.

Robert Reuben was the eldest son, brilliant intellectually, quiet and delicate-looking. Unlike most Brownings he lacked the ability to pro-

Family group of six of Reuben's children c. 1888.
Left to right, standing: WILLIAM DOODUM THOMAS HENRY, seated: ELIZABETH MICHAEL CHRISTINA
Robert Reuben had died in 1887 and Margaret had gone to Mauritius.

Afternoon tea-party in garden of 'Penhelig' 1880? Certainly after Reuben's death in 1879.
Left to right: Maid-servant and man-servant waiting on MICHAEL, seated at small table. LOUISA (Doodum) seated, MARGARET standing and CHRISTINA seated at larger table. Cook standing on right.
Elizabeth and Thomas in Paris?

ject an image and so was remembered by few who met him, including the poet. An aunt said he was protective towards his baby sister Mary Louise and cared for her in his house in Putney. He proved his father's will on December 20, 1879, and died a bachelor in 1887 before he reached the age of forty.

Michael Browning acted as the practical head of the family after his father died. He worked in the Rothschild Bank, for which he seemed destined from birth, having been presented with a clock as the result of an important meeting in Paris connected with the Brownings and the Rothschilds. He lived in the house called 'Woodyates', which Reuben left his four daughters, in Estcourt Road, Wandsworth, which became the family home for him and the girls after Reuben's death in 1879. He was sociable and enjoyed entertaining at home. William Hixon would join him for a drink at weekends.

Christina blamed the intrusion of a difficult brother-in-law, John Horne, for Michael's untimely death as a bachelor aged forty-three.

William went to Canada to make his fortune but passed away within

THOMAS HENRY BROWNING 1851–1893
Son of Reuben Browning. Born August 2, 1851.
Married Carrie Lovell in Croydon.
Died in Willesden May 1893, leaving three sons under the age of twelve:
(1) THOMAS, went to South Africa with twin son and daughter, (2)
MICHAEL, married a Miss Strauss (no children) died 1957, (3) ROBERT
SEYMOUR, later of Alexandria, Egypt.
Buried in Croydon.

hours of his return home in 1889 at the age of thirty-four. He is buried with his brother Thomas Henry in Shirley, Croydon.

Thomas Henry was my grandmother's favourite brother, who spent much time in Paris living it up. He swore to be 'a bachelor gay' but fell in love with Carrie Lovell, married her but died aged only forty-one in 1893, leaving three sons under twelve. He was buried with his brother William in Croydon. His eldest son Thomas went to South Africa to settle, and had two children Thomas and Doreen, and died in 1954. He had a grandson Robert Browning. Michael, the second son, married a Greta Strauss, cousin of the composer's family. They had no children. Michael was a prolific letter-writer and followed the example of his great-aunts Sarah and Louise by corresponding with all the members of the family far and wide. He lived in Addiscombe Road Croydon where he died in 1957.

The youngest son, *Robert Seymour*, was Captain in the Merchant Navy, in the Royal Navy in the 1939 war and was for twenty-five years in the Egyptian Government Service. His house in Bexhill-on-Sea, Sussex, was called 'Ras-el-tin' after his house in Alexandria, Egypt, where he lived with his family. He had a son, Commander Robert Browning, and a daughter Jennifer who married Wing Commander Breese. He died in December 1968. He said his mother Carrie wrote words to some of Christina Browning's music and that it was published by Leonard Gautier in 1901. He corresponded with Dr. Armstrong of the Armstrong Browning Library in Waco and in 1966 he, I and Michael Browning's widow held our own little ceremony in Poet's Corner to lay a wreath on the poet's grave on the anniversary of his death, December 12, during the Westminster Abbey Thousand Year celebration. I asked him to say a few words and had the Verger record the event in the Official Records of the Abbey. It was a truly merry Browning occasion.

Margaret. As there was an interval of several years between Christina and Margaret, Christina was adult when Margaret and her two younger sisters had lessons with a governess called Miss Fothergill. Margaret was serious, industrious, independent, well-behaved and clever. She was musical and from her finishing school in Paris learned the social graces. These qualified her for the position of governess to a family of social standing in Mauritius, where she was married to John Horne in 1886. She was known to the poet and had several Browning heirlooms as wedding presents. In 1893 John Horne received his 'congé', and they came home to England in 1891. They lived at 'Wood-yates' of which she was legal mistress but he remained the uninvited guest and the rest of the family felt they could not welcome him. A domestic crisis followed, and to this Christina attributed the death of Michael. Mr. and Mrs. Horne moved to Jersey, where she was widowed and herself died during the German occupation in the 1939–45 war. She was there visited by a neighbour whose daughter supplied the following memory of 1939 when Margaret was well over eighty years of age: 'I should say that she had been very good-looking in her day with a striking resemblance to your grandmother Kate Parks. She was very deaf and used one of the old earhorns. She entertained another old lady who was also deaf and it was quite a sight to see them both with the two earhorns reaching across the tea-table. The magnification of the sound through the earhorns was critical, since when speaking into the mouthpiece one was liable to get the instruction, "Don't shout! I'm not deaf!"

Her friend the Dean of Jersey died in 1938, the Rev. Atteyo died in Germany 1939–45, and her Doctor Oliver died in Germany 1939–45, so contacts with Mrs. Horne would be almost nil. She was rather a lonely old woman and my mother used to visit her every day. We used to take her out regularly two or three times a week. Her rooms were very Victorian and overcrowded with treasures. For her everyday tea she used Crown Derby china and a magnificent silver tea set, even when she was alone. She possessed a wonderful lot of jewellery of which the most beautiful and valuable was a set of emeralds and diamonds (ring, brooch and pendant necklace) which had been passed down to her.

She liked flowers/Mauritius/a little whisky or sherry. She was very fond of Frank Parks, Kate Parks' son (Sarianna's grandson), but he shocked her by being too modern. He once wore sandals without socks when visiting her!

She disliked cats, dogs, young people in general. On returning from a walk along the Havre des Pas: "My walk was quite spoilt ... pah! had to keep my face turned to the wall ... pah! half naked bodies all over the place ... pah!"

She wore ankle length clothes, carried a muff in winter. In summer she had a parasol and hats covered with fruit and flowers and feathers and wore a velvet throat band with a brooch. She was a tall woman with an upright stately carriage ... Furniture: she had no mirrors in the bathroom. It was indecent to see one's body. A mirror was in the hall and bedroom. A four-poster bed (no curtains). In the lounge a large portrait of her husband on the wall and a smaller framed photograph on an occasional table showed a man with full beard and side-

ROBERT SEYMOUR BROWNING
Youngest son of Thomas Henry Browning (1851–1893).
First cousin to my father and to the poet. Retired to Sussex where he named his house 'Ras – El – Tin' after his house in Alexandria, Egypt, where he was in Government service for twenty-five years, having previously been a Captain in the Merchant Navy.
In 1939 left Egypt to join the Royal Navy, being in R.N.R.

boards with stiff collar and stock with a large pin. A Victorian suite with wooden frame, several odd chairs and a rocker, hassocks with petit point tops and one with beads. China cupboards and a cheval table in gilt. Ornaments and pictures without number' (Stella Bartlett).

Her accommodation consisted of first floor flat. Large lounge, two

ELIZABETH BROWNING, 'Lizzie' 1859–1942
As she looked in the poet's lifetime when she was a frequent visitor to 19 Warwick Crescent.

Courtesy of Nora Collings

bedrooms, kitchenette and bathroom, in Plaisance Road, St. Helier, Jersey.

'She left a note that her grandmother Jane Smith was said to have been related to the Seymours, and was second cousin to Lord Macartney, ambassador to China, whose dinner service passed into Reuben's family, and to her on her marriage. Sir F. J. Furnivall mentioned he had eaten grapes from these plates. Two of them were given to Robert Seymour (Browning) as a wedding present' (*Browning Society Notes*, Vol. 3 No. 3, 'Talking of the Brownings').

Elizabeth, my grandmother, known as Lizzie, was born on July 10, in 1859 and was the poet's favourite of Reuben's children. She was always bursting with the particular ingredient of Browning vitality, enthusiasm, zest for life and sense of humour, combined with a love of people, individually or in company. She was tall with very white skin, red-gold hair and blue eyes. My cousins said the room appeared to light up when she entered and all attention was focused on her, so that at the At-homes, although perhaps not the most accomplished singer or performer on a musical instrument (she played the piano), she was always the most entertaining and remembered. She brought to the occasion a sense of fun, with impromptu dressing-up and miming famous people, or even the gypsies so admired by Robert, telling fortunes from tea-leaves in cups, or by reading palms. She said she used to make up yarns as she went along, but at times when she was carried away and said something really dramatic, there would be a blanching of faces and look of shock, and the revelation that what she said was perfectly true! She went to Paris for 'finishing' and told of her escapades there, escaping through the bedroom window for the excitement of a secret rendezvous with a beau whom she had met when chaperoned at a Paris ball.

For the balls, she and her sisters or cousins would be called for by carriage. They would have posies delivered for their nosegay holders, wear long white gloves and carry a fan. Fan language was taught at the finishing school. She had her own companion-chaperone, Clothilde, and she had programme-cards for dances which were always fully booked at the beginning of the ball. I have a coral and gold necklace and ear-ring set in a jewel case of navy-blue velvet, initialled in gold 'E.B. Paris', from that time, and some of her fans. She had letters to show that the poet took an especial interest and looked after her secretly after the death of her father. When she left 'Woodyates' after the quarrel with Christina, she married Dr. Cornelius Deacon and lived in Hastings in the summer and Chelsea in the winter. Dr. Deacon was in practice with Dr. Kelly in new electrical therapy in Portman Square, W.1. She was widowed. Her second husband was John Chamberlain with whom she travelled to Sydney, Australia.

My recollections of her are very clear. In 1928 when I was five

CLOTHILDE SASSON
Photographed in Paris August 3, 1881. Inscribed on the back 'To my dear Lizzie with my best love Clothilde Sasson'.

she came from Sydney to look after me and my nine-year-old sister Sybil in Melbourne while my parents were in Tasmania where my father was lecturing. Her hair was still deep gold although she was nearly seventy, and her eyes clear blue in her pale, finely wrinkled but unblemished skin. She looked tall and was slim with perfect carriage as she glided about the house. She spoke very quietly, since a lady does not raise her voice when speaking.

She always wore a full-length skirt, hitched up on one side with a brooch, to reveal an under-skirt. When indoors she had a lace head-piece pinned to back curls, and when she went out of doors she donned a squashed velvet musty-smelling toque (I think she must have kept all her clothes in mothballs), over which she drew a mesh veil which covered her face and was drawn into her throat. She was well-known to high Church of England dignitaries (she regularly marched me off to the services) and was invited by the Governor to attend garden parties at Government house and other official functions.

Although very gifted musically, she had no talent for domesticity or the culinary arts. The very first meal she served in my parents' absence was an evil-smelling glue-like substance which she called 'soup'. Sybil and I could not bear it under our noses, let alone taste the concoction, so that when a heaven-sent visitor called her away, we disposed of it down the kitchen sink. On her return she said, 'What, finished already? You must be hungry!' and she ladled out more! Our good upbringing forbade us to complain, so we held our breath, shut our eyes, and gulped it down as we took medicine or the nightly dose of syrup-of-figs or castor-oil, administered at bedtime since it was fashionable to keep 'regular' in health habits in those days.

She appeared strict but must have been very kind as she promised us breakfast in bed the next morning as a treat. We awoke bright and very much earlier than usual in anticipation of the event, but the hours seemed to pass and it did not materialise, so we raised a chant:

'Lazy lie-a-bed Lizzie,
Hunger is making us dizzy!'

which grew louder and louder until, hoarse and exhausted, we lay still in our beds. Soon Grandmama appeared with a tray. Very quietly she said, 'You would have had your breakfast earlier, but I was distracted by Australian street-urchins shouting in a most unseemly manner. I am pleased *you* do not raise your voices so! If you did I would not feel disposed to bring you breakfast in bed!'

I was my grandmother's constant companion as my sister was a book-worm in my father's library, which was the largest private library in Australia. She was happy telling stories of dear Cousin Robert, and I laughed at her accounts of the days at 'Penhelig' and Warwick Crescent. She was enchanting when she was old, so she must have been all that older cousins said she was when she was young, and today would have been a star in the theatrical world. She had brought many valuable mementos and Browning heirlooms and letters to Australia with her. Her son sold the three least important letters to the State Library of Australia, and a Browning ring with a lock of hair he gave to Robert Jardine Browning as security for a loan. Her intimate letters from the poet, which he wrote to her regularly after the death of Reuben, and an album containing family photographs including some taken of her with Robert, were burned in two fires which ravaged our Melbourne homes. Some photographs and signed books were in her home in Sydney. We came to England in 1930. These remaining treasures were parcelled up and sent to me after her death in November 1942, but the mail-boat was sunk.

Only one parcel arrived, sea-stained, but containing a miniature of Thomas Browning painted on ivory in a brooch framed in silver; an heirloom of my great-great-grandfather's hair entwined under glass, set in ebony and gold and framed with seed pearls; several loose photographs of the family, but not of her nearest relatives; and pawn tickets for rings which I endeavoured to redeem without success. Two Browning rings – cornelian stones set in Italian gold, given by Robert to Reuben – were held safe for us in England.

A letter from her landlady in Sydney said that she died in peace in hospital where they knew that she was a lady, and a relative of the famous poet, so they treated her accordingly.

Her letters to me showed that her last years were spent in loneliness (her only son, my father had died four years earlier), and in abject poverty, having to carry buckets of cold water from an outside tap to an upstairs single bed-sitting room. She had written poems and letters to me constantly, convinced that I would tell the family story one day. At the time I smiled disbelievingly at the idea, but she must have had a premonition that my older sister would die young and not be interested in the family, and that I would be the only one to report her accounts of the poet.

Mary Louise, the youngest child, was always known as Doodum, perhaps because she always remained child-like, quiet, well-behaved and delicate in health. She was protected by her eldest brother Robert

Reuben who could sympathise with her, being gentle of nature and delicate in health himself. She lost the use of her legs in middle age. After the death of Robert Reuben she stayed with her brother Michael and her sisters Christina and Elizabeth at 'Woodyates'. When 'Wood-yates' was sold, she and Christina stayed with Jemima's son's family,

MARY LOUISE, 'Doodum'
Youngest daughter of Reuben. Fair hair, blue eyes, delicate health. Called Doodum affectionately by her family since she was a baby.
Shared lessons with her sisters Margaret and Elizabeth.
Was cared for by William and Christina at various times.
After Christina's death she stayed with her aunts at Haverstock Hill. Took alcohol freely as a medicine.

the Hixons, at 'Kingsholme', 14 Aukland Hill, West Norwood. After that she was cared for by Carrie, the widow of Thomas Browning, at Norwood and Croydon. She was said to have taken alcohol for the relief of physical pain, and this accelerated her death.

These were the children living at 'Penhelig', Croydon, after Robert came back from Italy.

While Robert was abroad Reuben took charge of his financial affairs and investments in Italian stocks and bonds. They met on business as well as socially during Robert's visits home and to Paris. Reuben also kept the poet up-to-date with news, literature and the theatre. He informed the author of the successful reception (even favourably reviewed by Bernard Shaw) of the play *Colombe's Birthday*, performed first at the Haymarket Theatre, London, and then on tour with actress Helen Faucit in the lead. Helen Faucit, as Mrs. Martin, became great friends with the Brownings. In later years the poet was received as a guest at her home in Llangollen, where they used to attend service in the local old Norman church of Llantysilio. A brass plaque on the south wall records:

'In memory of Robert Browning, poet, who worshipped in this Church 1886, by his friend, Helen Faucit Martin.'

Another link was made with Wales when Elizabeth's brother Octavius Moulton-Barrett married Charlotte McIntosh on March 19, 1859 in the parish church of Aber, Caernarvon, not far from the Lewis family home. Brother Septimus Barrett was witness. This was two years after the death of Edward Moulton-Barrett who objected to the marriage of his children!

Reuben was very deaf, supposedly as the result of an accident with a cricket ball when he was young, and Robert gave the reason that he spoke loudly as Reuben's deafness. Several Browning descendants however became hard of hearing, Reuben's daughter Margaret, and his great-niece Kate Goodwin. Several friends of the family were also similarly afflicted, which presented no difficulties in communication with my grandmother who just mimed anything important she had to convey!

Out of doors, Reuben painted scenery in water-colours, and when he was indoors he wrote verbal sketches. I have a copy of one sketch (original in the Armstrong Browning Library) on the Death of Cher (a colleague in disguise) and what happens to him in the Central Criminal Courts of Heaven. If not the most brilliant example of Reuben's literary talent, at least it shows his originality in the telegrams which abound in Paradise! Several of Reuben's pamphlets on finance are listed in the British Library and there are many published congratulations on his treatises. I quote John Maynard in *Browning's Youth*, as a summary: '... anyone who troubles to dig out his polemics on financial subjects will find not dull technical treatises but eloquent pleas in which bank acts and interest per-cents stand next to citations from Aristotle, Plato, Lycurgus, Bishop Berkeley, or Locke. He seems to have had virtually as wide a general knowledge as Browning's father, with whom he loved to discuss historical matters over dinner.' The Browning biographer goes on to list Reuben's languages and other talents and abilities, not least his dramatic ability, and rightly attributes Browning-the-poet's interest in the dramatic monologue as perhaps originating from Reuben's interest in theatre and the mono-polylogues of Charles Matthews in particular. Reuben was able to portray characters verbally, as the poet's father was able to potray them in cartoon faces. (See *Browning's Old Schoolfellow* by Jack Herring.)

Reuben's long obituary (printed whole in *Browning Society Notes*, Vol. 3 No. 3, December 1973) ends with quoting from the eminent Dr. Kalisch, 'He had the soul of a gentleman, and the temperament of the philosopher. In the midst of practical pursuits, he never lost sight of the highest aims; and moving in the world, he preserved the purity of his nature intact.'

6 · The Poet Comes Home to England

The poet as he looked when living at 19 Warwick Crescent.

In 1861 after the death of Elizabeth, Robert brought their son Pen, aged twelve, to London where Elizabeth's sister Arabella had found accommodation temporarily in Chichester Road, Paddington, not far from her own home in Delamere Terrace. Soon afterwards they moved to 19 Warwick Crescent, where Robert was to set up home, with Sarianna as housekeeper, for twenty-five years, almost the rest of his life.

I was destined literally to walk in the family footsteps, for after walking the Camberwell paths daily to school, on my joining the Metropolitan Police as a uniformed police officer I was first posted to Paddington Green where I wandered across the border to Warwick Crescent and 'little Venice' – part of the Grand Union Canal over which the Browning house had a view; Robert and Pen were responsible for having trees put on the island. Then I was posted to Harrow Road Police Station as the only policewoman, my beats including Warwick Crescent, Chichester Road, the Grand Union Canal and Delamere Terrace. Fate decreed that I should not only walk the streets known to the Brownings for hours on end, but I actually had to make an official call personally at 19 Warwick Crescent, and was able to see the very same white marble fireplace before which my grandmother had had muffins with the poet.

It was to 19 Warwick Crescent that Reuben took his youngest three daughters, Margaret, Lizzie and Doodum, when they were small, and escorted other members of his family for soirées. My grandmother told how the poet took his little Lizzie on his lap to tell her stories and hug her. One of her favourite stories was how the poet came to write *The Pied Piper of Hamelin*, whose description he painted clearly in words:

> His queer long coat from heel to head
> Was half of yellow and half of red,
> And he himself was tall and thin,
> With sharp blue eyes, each like a pin,
> And light loose hair, yet swarthy skin,
> No tuft on cheek nor beard on chin,
> But lips where smiles went out and in; ...

so that actor William Macready's small invalid son Willie could illustrate it without difficulty. (An especial Pied Piper of Hamelin section of the Armstrong Browning Library, Waco, Texas, houses the original material connected with this poem and arranges exhibitions from time to time.) Lizzie and her sisters played with the animals while Reuben talked with the poet in the study. At this time Robert was rather like a Father Christmas, big and jolly and fond of giving presents or little mementos, unusual beetles or insects, small animals or scraps of verses with his own illustrations, but instead of reindeer, he had in the garden cackling geese, grass snakes and lizards, a mongoose and various other fauna; on his desk in the study he kept a pet owl which could be fed with small pieces of meat.

Robert had a hearty chuckle and a habit which could be construed as 'winking', but in reality was the spontaneous use of a built-in bi-focal mechanism, whereby he used his long-sighted and short-sighted eyes alternately, so that he did not require glasses. His eyes were of

PEN (on cushion) at Christchurch, 1869.

Clay model of a head in Pen's studio. The final cast of the bust, *Pompilia*, is in Wellesley College.

different intensity of colour too, as were my father's eyes. My grand mother was delighted that her son should inherit this distinctive Browning trait, which can clearly be seen in many of his photographs.

Sarianna was usually busy elsewhere in the house when the children were small and played in the garden. When the girls were old enough to take part in the At-homes they found Pen a most agreeable young man on the few occasions he was at home. He was ten years older than my grandmother and went to Oxford, to Christchurch, and later in life studied painting in Antwerp under the tuition of Jean-Arnould Heyermans, and studied sculpture under Rodin at his studio in Paris. Millais was responsible for introducing Pen to his first art master and recognised the real talent Pen had. He had eleven paintings exhibited at the Royal Academy of Art, and his sculpture exhibited in the Musée d'Art, Paris, and in Brussels, the nudity or near-nudity of some of Pen's work being too shocking for the London Royal Academy!

Photographs of Pen never did him justice or captured the personality of the young man. My grandmother found him to be tremendous fun and said he never had the credit due to his talents.

Family gatherings were most frequent at 'Penhelig', Croydon, and the garden setting in the photographs was familiar to Robert. My grandmother remembered the poet tucking her into bed. The Lewis family would swell the family for holidays and a descendant (Mrs. Jennie Lloyd-Hughes) remembers her mother telling her of a stay at 'Penhelig' when she was told to stay awake until the poet arrived to say 'Good-night'. She was proud to remember the occasion, in contrast with my dear friend Sir Charles Tennyson who knew that he was in the company of the poet on at least one visit to Faringford, Isle of Wight, but, try as he might, he was unable to recollect the occasion, much to his disappointment.

Reuben died in 1879 and his wife in 1881, and they were buried in the same grave in Shirley, Croydon. Elizabeth went to stay at coastal resorts or in Paris, and Robert, who had named Reuben and his children in his will, repaid some of the debt he felt he owed his uncle Reuben and took care of Elizabeth although she no longer visited him. The letters concerning her welfare are mentioned in a newspaper article as bearing 'ample evidence that the poet was generous-hearted to unfortunate relatives when it lay in his power' (*The Herald*, Melbourne, August 16, 1913).

Robert Browning died on December 12, 1889, and Elizabeth was not happy to share the life at 'Woodyates' with her sisters. After the death of Michael, she married Dr. Cornelius Deacon, who registered the birth of a son, Vivian Hereward Rowden Deacon, on August 9, 1895 at Chelsea, where they were living at the time. The Rosicrucian fraternity had an influence on this baby who was to carry on the Hermetic tradition of the Brownings and led a life which was an apt parallel to *Paracelsus* and which will fill a volume elsewhere.

7 · The Browning Hermetic Tradition in Australia

In 1907–1908 Reuben Browning's grandson, my father Vyvyan Deacon, as a young boy scout, travelled to Australia via India at the time that Annie Besant and Bishop Leadbeater were setting up their Theosophical headquarters in Adyar, India. He had already received publicity as a boy preacher on the sands at Broadstairs, and was custodian of the secret of the Christian Mysteries and the Rosy Cross. Before he was seventeen he was known as a lecturer for the Theosophical Society in Melbourne and on May 21, 1913, he was officially listed to speak on *Re-incarnation in Robert Browning's poetry*. On Saturday evening August 16, 1913, the whole front page of *The Herald*, Melbourne, was devoted to an article headed *Browning Letters; Relative of Poet*, and contains seven illustrations of letters and photographs which my grandmother had given my father. The article briefly lists the other Browning relatives in Australia, Cyrus Mason and Robert Jardine Browning and families, but more than half the article is devoted to the Law of Karma, Mesmerism, and on Browning theology, of which his young kinsman was an exponent. A reference is made to Rabbi Ben Ezra, then Vivian* Deacon is quoted:

> 'I tell you these scientists, these free-thinkers, these agnostics, these nothings-at-all, are all soul-hungry and tired – for want of a God. My intention is to form a Browning society somewhat on the lines of the Theosophists, but we will practise and study from the teaching in the poems. We shall endeavour to obtain a knowledge of God, not merely intellectual, but in every fibre of our being, so that we know He is.'

He continues to discuss astral travel and transcendental meditation and proclaims, 'I am a vegetarian, and have studied psychotherapeutics and practise total abstinence from alcohol and tobacco.'

*He changed his name from *Vivian* to *Vyvyan* after an eventful period as he felt the more y's the better!

The reporter was sufficiently impressed to write: 'Although talking with the fluency and confidence of middle age this young man, seemingly in the early twenties, is but eighteen years of age this month. Already he numbers leading theosophists among his friends, sceptics among his pupils, and enthusiasts among his followers.'

Robert Browning wrote a poem called *Mesmerism* – noted by Paul Turner in his edition of *Men and Women* as being but one single sentence throughout stanzas two to twenty inclusive, each stanza consisting of five lines! The poem tells of a woman being drawn through material objects to a loved one, through the powers of concentration. W. B. Yeats used this technique to experience love on the astral plane, and had discussed the subject with the poet himself. Today on mass media one hears people who believe that it will not be long before we are able to travel without motorised transport!

In 1914 my father was trained by Bishop Leadbeater in Theosophical and Rosicrucian practices. Leadbeater's books and Rudolf Steiner's books on Rosicrucianism and Free-masonry, although published many years after this time, reveal many of the subjects well known to the poet and my father as family tradition.

While in Sydney my father became a great friend of Norman Lindsay, head of the famous Australian literary family. They shared the study of Steiner and the Occult and my father developed into a very powerful spiritualist medium, whose gifts were admired by Norman Lindsay. Their secrets were kept safe, but about this time my father founded the Australian Order of Oriental Templars, which praised the Hymn of Pan of Aleister Crowley. Norman Lindsay's young sons, Jack and especially Phil, knew my father at this time and of the Pan Cult which developed on a social level. Robert Browning's poem *Pan and Luna* and references to Pan in his poem *Pheidippides* show the poet's belief in the sacred significance of the physical expression of love, and – in the latter poem – the value of the prize of family life, while the extent of his source material for the poems show that he knew very well the Pan tradition.

Norman Lindsay admired Browning; Jack Lindsay says his father's favourite poem was *Women and Roses*. I feel very much the significance of Jack Lindsay's Pan poem extending over twenty-four years, about the same span which covered the years between the poet's death and the time Jack Lindsay and my father discussed this subject in Sydney, and quite spontaneously Jack has linked up the tenuous threads in a spirit of the Eternal Now.

AUSTRALIAN NOON

Pan's noon on all. Even lovers
in midkiss stay.
The kiss faints, but the lips
do not move away
Silence is taut. The lark
is tombed in the sun.
Linnet and sparrow are secret,
everyone.

The Australian noon locks all, yet spreads out rising
into the skies, into the depth upon depth
of opening light. The continent is one
and all of us caught in the perfect moment of wholeness.
The light turns over and over, embracing the earth
in fertile rhythms that spin to the topless cone.
The great reflected image is turning, revolving, revealing
every curve and cave of mother-earth surrendered
to the penetrating all-pervasive sun.

No other noon like this. Here Pan
is terrible, yet smiles on man.
This moment of sheer union we knew.
It broke and left us once again
our separate selves, yet with the clue
that drew us through the engulfing maze
into that other space, the blaze
of joy and harmony anew.

The memories remain
and are enough. We move ahead,
led still by the involving thread,
through tangled struggles pledged to gain
the various earth and prove it good
in undemanding brotherhood;
yet stay in part where we began
in the stark timeless noon of Pan.

JACK LINDSAY

The first eight lines come from a lyric written in Sydney in May 1924;
the rest of the poem was written in September 1978 for the author.

My father's bizarre magical powers were frequently praised in the Australian press at a time when many spiritualist practices contravened the law. In 1928 a reporter challenged those powers in a libellous article. The result was a libel suit settled in my father's favour, with the award of unprecedented damages. Defending the losing side was a young advocate Robert Menzies, a future Prime Minister of Australia, with whom my father duelled verbally in court. There was mutual admiration. My father said that he increased Robert Menzies' appreciation of Browning, at that time. Imagine my delight on reading in the report of Sir Robert Menzies' funeral, that 'Sir Robert's old friend, the Very Rev. Fred McKay ... talked of the Menzies who recited Browning to stockmen and had them crowding to hear more.'

The impact of the Browning tradition in Australia was real!

I could go on ad infinitum to record the effect Browning had on people he met and their descendants. References to Browning worldwide render my doing so superfluous.

Rudolf Steiner says, 'All "theosophy" implies a knowledge of the spiritual world, and such knowledge has been attained in different ways at different epochs of man's history. The Rosicrucian way ... is the way suited to modern man in this age of world knowledge and individual freedom' (*The Theosophy of the Rosicrucian*).

Jowett wrote of Browning in his lifetime: 'It is impossible to speak without enthusiasm of his open, generous nature and his great ability and knowledge. I had no idea that there was a perfectly sensible poet in the world, entirely free from vanity, jealousy, or any other littleness, and thinking no more of himself than if he were an ordinary man.' (*Life and Letters of Benjamin Jowett* by Evelyn Abbott and Lewis Campbell, 1897).

I hope that I have helped people to see more of the real Browning, whose aim was to be as Christian as is humanly possible in the Western way of life into which he was firmly placed by Destiny.

Acknowledgements

Instinctively, and with encouragement from my grandmother I collected details of the larger Browning family. Our homes in Australia suffered two fires and our home in London was demolished by a land-mine in the Second World War. I had to make an especial effort to replace missing pictures from my photograph album by getting into touch with Browning relatives.

I am most indebted to Philip Kelley, whom I met in 1961 when he was organising the Elizabeth Barrett Browning Exhibition in St. Marylebone Library, one hundred years after her death. That he should know instantly who I was when I told him I was Reuben's descendant has never ceased to amaze me. His enthusiasm for the work I had done on the family tree inspired me to greater effort, and his practical help with information added much to my collection. I am sorry I have not had time to put to use the material he sent me on the old Dorset forebears, to compile a worthy companion and reference book for his Browning correspondence, of which *The Brownings' Correspondence: A Checklist*, by Kelley and Hudson has been published by The Browning Institute and Wedgestone Press; but all material I have stored for future reference.

I am conscious of many omissions from *My Browning Family Album*. A Miss Despard told me of her grandfather Henry Browning who was believed to be related to the poet. He was contemporary with him, composed music, knew Dickens's sister, had a rare book on a Masonic brotherhood and was involved in and well known in Masonry; and was known as Henry Browning of Threadneedle Street. But I have so far been unable to place him. I contacted the late Sir Vincent Baddeley, a distant cousin, but could add nothing to the information he provided for 'The Ancestry of Robert Browning the Poet' (*The Genealogists' Magazine*, Vol. 8 No. 1, March 1938). I have tried to confine my information to events contemporary with the poet or which would give a picture of the kind of human family background in which he was placed and of which he had constant knowledge. Because of destructive elements in my life my list of helpers of necessity is large but I must specifically thank the following: Mrs. Pearl Alexander for her notes on Fanny Mason; The Armstrong Browning Library, Director Dr. Jack Herring for his unique comments on Browning's poetry of which his knowledge is most profound, and Librarian Mrs. Betty Coley, for access to their Browning collection, including the Cyrus Mason manuscript, *Browning Kinsfolk*, Judith Berlin's *Browning and Hebraism*, many Browning letters, copies of *The Browning Newsletter* and other publications from which Dr. Herring has given me permission to quote, and for their interest in my work over the years in our mutual exchange of information; Stella Bartlett and Nana Bartlett for their memory of my great-aunt Margaret and Jersey, Mr. James Bentley, Mrs. Dorothy Biffo for her Aunt Kitty's photograph album with Althaus family pictures; Miss Catherine Browning ('Tip'), Mr Geoffrey Browning for photographs of Robert Shergold and family and his ancestor's book William Shergold's *History of the Huguenots*, now in St. Marylebone Library for reference, his continued support and assistance; Greta Browning (Mrs. Michael Browning) for photographs, books and information on the family; the late Captain Robert Seymour Browning for photographs and recollections; Mr. W. F. Baly, Yolanda, Vivienne, John and Lynne for their secretarial and practical assistance and John for his sketch of the Browning arms as used by the poet. Mr. Gerald Buckley for the photograph taken with Ben Travers. Mrs. Nora Collings and Mr. Norman Collings for their invaluable contribution on Jemima's family and for access to the unique family collection of Browning items and permission to reproduce photographs; *Dorset* and the Rev. Anthony Lane for permission to quote from his article 'the brownings at woodyates and pentridge' (sic) in *Dorset*, No. 28 1972; Mrs Dorothy Gwyther; the late Mrs. Kate Hamilton Parks for Mason family photographs; Miss Elsie Horstead and the Warburg Institute for access to books on Rosicrucian magic; Mrs. Jennie Lloyd-Hughes for the family photograph of Reuben Browning, information on the Lewis family and the gift of the family tea-pot and spoons, the tea-pot as seen in the photograph in the garden of 'Penhelig'; Mr. Brian Hulme and Susan for their reproduction of the William Shergold Browning arms; Mrs. Esme Laurence for information on descendants of Philip Mason; John Maynard for permission to quote from his *Browning's Youth* and encouragement to disagree publicly with statements on Browning should I feel so inclined! Miss Phyllis Mann for references to Browning ancestors; St. Marylebone

Library for allowing me access to the papers of Sir Vincent Baddeley; Mrs. Osyth Leeston of Murrays for her invaluable support, Mrs. June North for information on Shöndauer; Dr. William Peterson for information on family letters and permission to quote from Browning Institute Studies, Browning Institute, Inc.; Photocall and partner Mr. Brian Wetherill, M.M.P.A. for photographic reproduction on demand; Mrs. Joy Pye for Mason family information; Mr. John Riddle for his photograph of Woodyates; Mr. John Scarlett for information on his ancestor Cyrus Mason; Mrs. Sheila de Spon for items on Fannie Browning; Mrs. Hazel White for information on Browning descendants in New Zealand; Mr. John Woolford, Editor of Browning Society Notes (London) for permission to quote from published articles; friends and librarians too numerous to name who have aided me in gaining information which I may or may not have used.

A   **ROBERT BROWNING**

m. (1) Margaret Tittle   m. (2) Jane Smith

Robert   Margaret   William   Wm Shergold   Christina
m. Sarah   Morris   m. Louisa
Anne Wiedemann   Monsir

Robert
m. EB M-B

Robert (Pen)   Sarianna

Christina   Robt   Michael   William   Thomas   Margaret
(Violet Seymour)   Reuben   m. John Horn

                              Thomas Michael   Robert Seymour

B   **WILLIAM SHERGOLD BROWNING**
                              m. Louisa Mansir

William   John   Elizabeth   Robert Shergold   Louisa Jane
Mansir   Wace   Ann   m. Harriet C.   m. R. J. Dyke
                      m. B. Sly   Triquer

Robert Jardine   Harriet Elizabeth   Percy   Charles Dearmer   Arthur
m. Beatrice Lamb m. J. F. Firth   m. Maud Carr

Muriel   Charles   Winifred   Geoffrey   Ada   Eric
Maud   Robert   Ethel   Shergold   Louise   Basil
                       m. J. Anderson

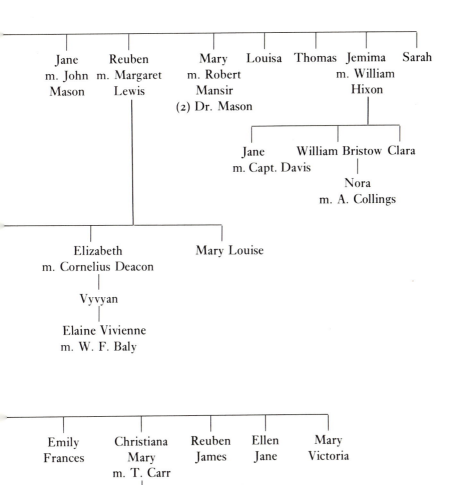

Jane
m. John
Mason

Reuben
m. Margaret
Lewis

Mary
m. Robert
Mansir
(2) Dr. Mason

Louisa

Thomas

Jemima
m. William
Hixon

Sarah

Jane
m. Capt. Davis

William

Bristow

Clara

Nora
m. A. Collings

Elizabeth
m. Cornelius Deacon

Vyvyan

Elaine Vivienne
m. W. F. Baly

Mary Louise

Emily
Frances

Christiana
Mary
m. T. Carr

Reuben
James

Ellen
Jane

Mary
Victoria

Louisa Maud
m. Charles D. Browning

C   **JANE ELIZA BROWNING**

m. John Mason

Reuben	Arthur	Eliza Jane	Cyrus
d. Bristol	d. New York	m. Ed Goodwin	m. Jessie Campbell
		(no family)	

Laura
m. M. McDonall

Barbara Constance
m. Alfred Scarlett

John

D   **REUBEN BROWNING**

m. Margaret Lewis

Christina	Robt	Michael	William
(Violet Seymour)	Reuben		

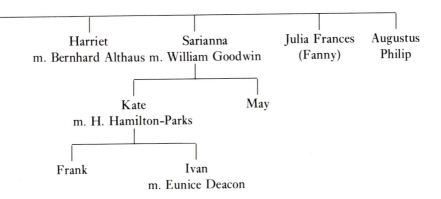

Harriet
m. Bernhard Althaus

Sarianna
m. William Goodwin

Julia Frances
(Fanny)

Augustus
Philip

Kate
m. H. Hamilton-Parks

May

Frank

Ivan
m. Eunice Deacon

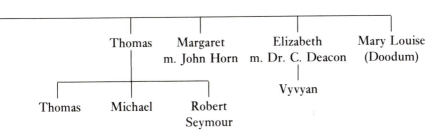

Thomas

Margaret
m. John Horn

Elizabeth
m. Dr. C. Deacon

Mary Louise
(Doodum)

Thomas

Michael

Robert
Seymour

Vyvyan